ENGLISH COTTAGE INTERIORS

ENGLISH COTTAGE INTERIORS

Hugh Lander & Peter Rauter

WEIDENFELD AND NICOLSON
LONDON

First published in Great Britain in 1989 by
George Weidenfeld & Nicolson Limited
91 Clapham High Street, London SW4 7TA

Designed by Lindsey Rhodes

Colour separations by Newsele Litho Ltd
Filmset by Tradespools Ltd, Frome, Somerset
Printed and bound in Italy by L.E.G.O., Vicenza

Half Title Page: SHROPSHIRE The triangular upstairs oriel window
of a Gothic semidetached cottage in Ludlow, dated 1842, proves an
ideal place to display a collection of old bottles. To make them easily
identifiable, those containing poisons were often made from bright
blue or green glass. They were also ribbed or made in distinctive
shapes so that they could provide a warning by touch alone.

Title Page: CORNWALL Cornwall's fishing villages are full of tiny,
stone-built cottages which huddle cheek to cheek on either side of
steep lanes leading down to secret harbours. This one, on The Lizard
peninsula, would have been typical fifty years ago. After several
decades of modernizing zeal the fetching simplicity seen here is rarely
encountered. Until the new Building Regulations of 1985 were
introduced, repairs often involved raising ceiling heights. Fortunately
that is no longer a requirement, but to this day new upstairs floors
with joists as far apart as these are frowned upon by building control
officers – more's the pity!

ACKNOWLEDGEMENTS

I should like to thank all the owners, organizations and individuals who have helped to make this book possible. They have been unstintingly generous in so many ways. The first thank you must be to all those kind and hospitable people who have allowed me to look at their cottages and have taken such pains to explain and discuss the histories and details of their homes. Next, my profound gratitude goes to all the owners and tenants of the many cottages which we actually photographed for inclusion in the book. Most of them were living in the buildings while this sometimes disruptive operation was carried out. In a number of cases we have organizations to thank, who showed great restraint in allowing us to research and take pictures when they had visiting members of the public to consider at the same time.

One of the principal pleasures in researching this book has been the opportunity to make so many new friends. Never did they suggest that the invasion of their lives was an unwelcome imposition. They gave solace to the weary cottage hunter in the form of coffee, drinks, meals and sometimes the use of the spare room for the night. On one occasion, a charming lady, first encountered the previous evening, lent me an entire timber-framed cottage in one of the most architecturally exciting market towns in England.

To find sufficiently charismatic cottages it was often necessary to adopt methods which would be well understood by the private detective or the racecourse punter, gleaning leads and tip-offs in pubs, shops and restaurants, even by stopping blameless citizens in the street or by knocking on likely doors. If one needed proof that the English are, by and large, an extraordinarily warmhearted and outgoing nation, this would have been the way to do it. On a more formal basis, friends and acquaintances came up with vastly useful contacts and introductions. The promise of a delectable cottage in one village would frequently find me ensconced by the fire at ten o'clock at night in another place miles away. I shall never know if some of the cottage owners were gracefully concealing their chagrin at this state of affairs. If so, I am all the more grateful to them.

Lastly, I should like to thank Felicity Luard, my editor at Weidenfeld and Nicolson, for her patience, encouragement and professionalism. To her these qualities may seem to be the natural requirements of a demanding job; but no author is likely to underestimate their importance.

AUTHOR'S NOTE
As many owners preferred that their cottages should not be identified, a county heading has been used to indicate the first picture of each cottage.

KENT

The newel stair of this early-to-mid-16th-century building in Kent, not far from Headcorn, is mysterious but infinitely inviting. Who would not take pleasure in ascending those winding stairs on their way to bed? The cupboard door, made from three broad oak planks, is fixed together with large hand-made nails. The fish-tail strap hinges are also attached, as they should be, with nails and not screws. (See also pages 76–7.)

CONTENTS

INTRODUCTION

The parlour of this post office cottage (pages 93–7), has a fireplace which is 18th century in flavour. The proportions and use of the mantel shelf to form a cornice above a block-decorated frieze suggest a countrified version of something from one of the 18th-century pattern books, though the distinctive triple flush bead around the framing of the side cupboards makes the period from 1800 to 1830 a more likely bet. An additional board has been superimposed on the original mantelpiece, perhaps to accommodate the clock. A painting of the post office cottage, with its thatched roof, has been framed in a firescreen which hides the modern grate.

O n warm summer evenings the top of the stable door is left open. Imperceptibly, the colours of the garden fade until only the whites of mock orange and night-scented stocks can be picked out of the gathering darkness. The heavy, honeyed aroma of the Etoile de Hollande rose over the door is caught on the air and lost, and caught again. It is so quiet that the sound of a chain being dropped over a gatepost can be heard from the end of the cart track. The cadence of conversation becomes muted and reflective. As facial expressions dissolve into obscurity, long pauses, containing other and irrelevant thoughts, hover unspoken in the spaces.

We are reluctant to turn on the lights, but when we do a familiar scene from twentieth-century cottage life is revealed: whitewashed stone walls, a low ceiling of boards and painted joists, a flagstoned floor with a Caucasian kelim in front of the huge open hearth with its summer dressing of wild flowers in a stone crock. A big dresser stacked with blue-and-white cups and saucers, mugs, and earthenware casseroles dominates one wall. The scrubbed pine table bears the detritus of yet another simple meal of bolognese, home-made bread, Cabernet Sauvignon wine, and salad, artfully seasoned with garden herbs.

On the bookshelves beside the fireplace are piled the compact-disc player and video machine. A watercolour painting, perhaps by David Cox, portrays another cottage, in another time. It is wedged into a barren hillside, with a not too terrifying mountain rising behind it. A girl in a long skirt is standing near the low doorway of this romantic and weather-beaten croft. She is holding a wicker basket, her arm hooked through the handle. The scene has a magical freshness about it. You can smell the woodsmoke from the chimney and visualize the sparse, but clean and orderly kitchen which lies behind the shaded oblong of the open door.

We are dreaming, of course. The well-appointed, comfortable, bookish and civilized rural simplicity of today's cottage interior, with its potpourri and polished stick-back chairs is a triumph of casual cleanliness and informed taste. The inside of the nineteenth-century hovel was quite probably a scene of dirt, poverty and disease, where the occupants, according to their degree of luck, skill and industry, wrested what pleasure and sustenance they could from an unforgiving land.

England abounds in pretty cottages and there are villages so picturesque, in the wider sense of the word, that they have become as familiar to the public eye as any of the famous show-business beauties we are accustomed to see trailing their expensive luggage through international airports. While a good deal more enduring, the cottages of England are, alas, as prone to vulgar and clumsy artifice. There is quite enough heavy-handed over-restoration to be seen and never more so than *inside* those beguiling walls of brick and stone and lopsided timber framing.

This book is not intended as a critique which tears apart the infelicities of those many buildings which have been horribly abused. Nor is it meant to be a work of architectural history, tracing the development of the English cottage from the first crude circular huts to the neat and flimsy mini-villas of the Victorian era. It is essentially a book which has been designed to give pleasure and perhaps inspire the reader by demonstrating the beauty and simplicity of cottage interiors where texture and authentic detail have been lovingly preserved and enhanced. It is a picture gallery of the best that can be found, whatever the date or genre.

During more than a year of research, which has taken me from the northern extremities of Blennerhasset and Berwick-upon-Tweed to Felixstowe, Lyme Regis and The Lizard peninsula, I became accustomed to the local inhabitants' most persistent question. 'What', they would say, 'exactly do you mean by a cottage?' It rapidly dawned upon me that I did not exactly know the answer. With desperate sophistry I would intone about size and purpose, the low estate of the inhabitants, of cots and of cotters. But it became clear that a strict definition of the word was almost impossible and most probably undesirable. We all knew what a cottage was anyway; it was precisely the kind of building which each one of us had in his or her mind's eye as the essential archetype. For each person it was something slightly different, and contemporary sources show that it has always been so. In the 1790s, delightful Fanny Burney and her aristocratic French émigré husband, M. d'Arblay, built what she firmly refers to as a 'cottage' and 'our Lilliputian home'. It cost £1,300 and had numerous small rooms, including an entrance hall, three reception rooms, a kitchen, scullery, library, four bedrooms and a dressing room.

Most of the entrancing and evocative pictures which Peter Rauter has taken, as he followed in my footsteps, are indeed of small buildings which were built for peasants or artisans. But we have included a certain number of farmhouses and small hall-houses simply because we could not resist their charms. In one or two cases, a building has been photographed because it embodies some special feature which was common to the way of life or methods of construction in a past age.

There is little doubt that the majority of early dwellings which we now call cottages were occupied by people of a somewhat greater prosperity than ordinary craftsmen or rural labourers. Few of the tiny wattle-and-daub hovels which the latter built on corners of common land, or wherever they could find a site where they might be permitted to settle, have survived. Successive land clearances at different points in history meant the abandonment of these squalid, leaking and draughty dwellings. Most have just sunk back into the ground from which their essential materials were so laboriously won.

Many of the cottages we see were the homes of yeoman farmers, master craftsmen, minor professional men, tradesmen and even merchants. The original concept of a one-room, single-storey building, thrown up in a night with a fire burning in the middle of the floor by next morning to establish occupation, is not so far short of the mark for some of the more substantial buildings. These might equally be described as improvements on the theme of the one- or two-room shanty, where the animals lived cheek by jowl with the family, or as scaled-down versions of the semi-feudal hall-houses of the gentry.

The inside of most small houses before the sixteenth century consisted of one or two ground-floor rooms, roughly partitioned from each other to include a through-passage leading from front to back. The 'hall' or main living room would be open to the roof, and smoke from the central hearth found its way out either through the thatch itself, or by means of an opening in the gable or near the eaves. In long-houses, the farm animals occupied a byre at the lower end of a cottage built on a sloping site. The byre had a central gutter in the floor which drained out through the gable wall. More sophisticated small houses would not include shelter for the animals, but would have a main open 'hall' or kitchen-living room, with a cross-passage and a couple of service or storage rooms on the other side. Above these could be a rudimentary sleeping chamber reached by a ladder stair.

By the middle of the sixteenth century the better kind of small hall-house might have a chimney stack instead of an open central hearth, and a newel staircase winding around the chimney breast or a straight flight of stairs along a back wall. There could even be a newel stair housed in a semicircular projection called a caracole. At the end of the century people began to insert first floors in open halls and this practice continued into the seventeenth century. Chimney stacks were frequently introduced at this time.

By the end of the seventeenth century, many little houses and cottages had two or more downstairs rooms, plus a linhay or lean-to. There might be a simple timber-framed staircase boxed in with studs and boards, a big main hearth in the living room and, quite frequently, a lesser hearth in the other main downstairs room, which served as a parlour. Bedrooms were nearly always tucked into the roof space, with sloping ceilings, and often the window sills almost touched the floor.

The eighteenth century saw minimal development of this system – slightly higher ceilings and gradually a greater attention to symmetry in design – culminating in the box-like brick, stone or timber-framed cottages of the late-eighteenth and nineteenth centuries,

WILTSHIRE

The Elizabethan and Stuart periods saw the modernization of most of our surviving medieval hall-houses. The first requirements were a chimney stack and an upper floor. This bedroom has been formed in the roof space of an open hall with arch-braced trusses, which must originate from around the end of the 15th century. The white painted door, however, is of the two-panel Queen Anne pattern, which frequently had quadrant moulding on one side and nailed H-L hinges.

with their small-paned timber casements or double-hung sash windows. Rooms remained fairly cramped, and staircases often led straight up from the central entrance passage opposite the front door.

Despite these less rudimentary cottages, which became available in the eighteenth and nineteenth centuries, much of the rural population continued to live in the same dismal shacks, or tiny, crude, stone or brick buildings as before. Many still had no proper fireplaces and any upstairs sleeping quarters might amount to no more than a loft which covered part of the main room, reached by a ladder. The ground floor would usually be of beaten earth or perhaps grip, a mixture of lime, coal ash and clay. Only the rather better cottages had bricks, pamments, stone flags or tiles.

Any investigation of cottage life, from medieval times to the Georgian era, reveals few changes as far as the poor are concerned. Whether you consult the drawings of Hogarth, Morland or Cruikshank the picture remains the same as it would have been before the Dissolution of the Monasteries in 1536. The consistent theme in all accounts is one of disrepair, overcrowding, minimal possessions, the absence of sanitation and, at best, primitive and often polluted water supplies. The inhabitants had four overriding concerns: they had to work, they needed a fire to keep warm, they required food and, when it became dark, they slept in whatever makeshift beds they could contrive.

All these privations applied to the poorest elements of society, but there were people who could be counted as cottage dwellers who fared a good deal better. Grander buildings slipped down the social scale and afforded more spacious and better constructed accommodation. Farms and manor houses were sometimes subdivided to house two or three families, and the internal proportions of these buildings changed accordingly. Matchboard or muntin-and-plank partitions were inserted, new front doors replaced windows, additional staircases might be added and extra fireplaces and flues constructed.

In areas where the wool trade dominated the economy, cottages were built for weavers which provided a large open space on the top floor, where looms could be set up. These workshops were lit by four-, five-, or even six-light mullioned windows.

In the eighteenth and nineteenth centuries, many cottages were built by landowners to house their estate workers. These tended to be designed in fanciful styles which reflected architectural fashions of the moment. The cult of the 'picturesque' brought about a plethora of gate lodges, gamekeepers' cottages, coachmen's quarters, and the like. Often Gothic in inspiration, they had the advantage of being made from superior materials to coherent and properly thought out plans. The fact that the inhabitants might be obliged to live in two circular or octagonal rooms does not seem to have worried the landlords, provided their good works made the landscape more amusing. However inconvenient these buildings may have been, they still provided new and decent shelter for people whose plight could otherwise have been much worse.

Self-employed tradesmen and craftsmen frequently had cottages which adjoined their places of work. A miller might have a cottage which was attached to or even constructed as part of the mill itself. A blacksmith would have his forge nearby or in a lean-to addition. Some cottages also served as village bakeries. The oven backed onto a main wall, or occasionally might be in the principal room of the dwelling itself and amount to no more than a larger and better form of the normal oven behind the hearth. Turnpike-keepers, lock-keepers and ferrymen tended to have specially devised windows, hatches or stable doors which gave them a view of whoever might be approaching.

It would be easy to assume that the rural idyll which the better off cottager might be supposed to enjoy was, in fact, the reality. How pleasant to live with the fresh air on your face, the peace of the countryside and the fruits of the field near at hand? There was some truth in that for the man in steady employment, phlegmatic and frugal of disposition, with an iron constitution and a smattering of education. For others the mean conditions, lack of opportunity and boredom must have been intolerable.

The subdivision of the average rural cottage was a straightforward business. The overall size of the building and the period of its construction might make for some variety, but essentially there would be a main kitchen-living room (or 'hall'), a second ground-floor room, which could be a parlour. A lean-to at the back acted as a dairy, larder or scullery, or some combination of the three. Frequently the lean-to also contained a copper and served as a wash-house; but more often this was placed in a small ancillary building, sometimes with a woodshed alongside it. Another vital cottage outbuilding was the pig-sty, for most families kept a pig if they could manage to do so.

The shell of the building was normally one of four main types of construction. It could be of stone, brick, timber framing with wattle-and-daub infill, or of cob. In some parts of England (especially the Southeast), eighteenth- and nineteenth-century cottages were made of regular softwood studwork covered outside with weatherboards or tiles. Where good materials were scarce or expensive they might be combined, as in the case of the brick-and-flint cottages to be found in counties like Buckinghamshire.

External walls were treated internally with a thick application of plaster, which was made from clay, reinforced with cow hair and the sparing use of some lime to help bind the mixture together. Other reinforcement materials were used as well as cow or ox hair, including chopped straw and reeds, horse and goat's hair. The plaster was applied in one or two coats and finished with limewash. When you peel the rotting wallpaper off damp cottage walls, you will find that coats of limewash have built up over the years to some considerable thickness and, by careful dissection, you may be able to count how many have been applied. In some cottages, the limewash was brushed straight onto the stonework. Partition walls were made from softwood or hardwood stud framing with riven or sawn laths nailed on to form a base and key for the plaster. Ceilings, when they existed at all, were made in much the same way, but in later cottages they were frequently of thin tongued-and-grooved softwood matchboarding, which might have very narrow flush beads run along the edges of the boards.

In the more civilized eighteenth- and nineteenth-century buildings, the inner faces of external walls, especially if they were of very uneven stone, could be framed in timber to which lath and plaster were then applied. In all but the more refined cottages, the door frames were of morticed, tenoned and pegged scantling and the door itself was hung on wrought-iron strap or T hinges. These were invariably nailed and not screwed until well on in the nineteenth century.

Doors were made from vertical boards with two or three other boards in the form of 'ledges' nailed across them to hold everything together. The nails were banged right through and clenched over to prevent them pulling out. Door latches were employed in most cottages since they were cheaper than a lock or rim latch. Timber latches were normally operated by a string or leather thong passed through a hole in the boards. Iron latches had a metal lever and the Norfolk type had a vertical iron handgrip attached to a thin fixing plate. Early iron latches of the sixteenth and seventeenth centuries consisted of an iron handgrip, with a thumb latch lever at the top. Some simple doors had nothing more than a timber bolt contained by three iron or wood staples, and in many cases the door might have a block of wood nailed to it as a pull.

The timber first floor was usually of hardwood until about the eighteenth century, and was always of that material when the building was of traditional oak frame construction. Where the span from front wall to back was short, the joists were sufficient to bear the weight, but over a broader span spine beams might be placed along the length of the cottage. They in turn supported the smaller joists on which the wide oak or elm boards were laid. Often cottage joists and boards were visible in the downstairs rooms and by the end of the eighteenth century they were normally painted. When not painted they were either limewashed or whitewashed, but oak floors might be left in their natural state. However, since light was at a premium, the general tendency was to whitewash everything. Many rough cottages had plaster ceilings put in at some point in their history, and when exposed beams and joists are seen today they often bear the marks and nail holes of the laths.

It was not until well on in the seventeenth century that even the grandest cottage would be expected to have a framed timber staircase with strings, treads and risers, although these had been in use in farms and manor houses for some time. The usual cottage stair-case was made of tapering timber or stone treads, winding in a spiral in any convenient corner available. Since most original cottage stairs have long since been replaced, it is worth looking for the telltale curved depression in an internal corner which indicates how the builders robbed space from the wall to accommodate the stair treads. Although normally to be found in more important buildings (and its presence may be a clue to a decline in status) the mast-newel stair was a further option. This was made from a single tall spar, with the narrow ends of the timber winders socketed into it. Simpler variations of this process can be found in Georgian cottages, where treads were sometimes housed into a short rectangular post.

The steep ladder staircase was made in a single straight flight, without risers. It was the sort of thing you might now expect to see in a mill, brewery, barn or warehouse. In some Northumberland miners' cottages the sleeping loft or upper floor was sometimes reached by an ordinary ladder, and such arrangements have been used within living memory. Occasionally, early cottages (pre-1700 or so) had solid timber baulks as winders, which were laid directly onto a rubble fill. Such treads could equally be of stone or brick.

Cottage windows were seldom glazed when of the poorest variety, until at least the end of the seventeenth century. The window would be little better than a hole in the wall with a rudimentary oak frame and vertical wooden bars or mullions. These were secured with shutters. Often a lattice of laths or wicker was used and, instead of glass, an oiled cloth was fixed across it. Many nineteenth-century cottages and estate buildings had timber glazing bars set in a lattice pattern; cast-iron glazing bars were also popular. When early cottages did have lead-glazed windows, few would be openable and glass was far too expensive for the average labourer, who would stuff rags into missing panes instead. Curtains were improvised from sacks or any piece of old cloth that could be found.

Beautifully made timber-mullioned windows with iron opening casements and small leaded panes can often be assumed to show that the so-called cottage was formerly the home of somebody a good deal wealthier than a farm labourer. All the same, it must be remembered that vast numbers of the rural poor inhabited buildings which had fallen on hard times. Certainly, contemporary drawings do show what appear to be glazed windows in poor hovels, but such evidence must be treated with caution.

Some internal cottage or farmhouse shutters dropped down between runners to floor level when the window was open, and were held up by inserting pegs in the frame when shut. Others ran back horizontally along the adjoining wall in a simple timber frame. Most shutters swung on iron hinges and were secured with a timber or iron bar.

It is very difficult to be sure when the practice of painting the insides of small cottages

West Sussex

The occupant of this wonderfully evocative old building in a little Sussex hamlet was born, like his five brothers, in the brass bedstead upstairs. From the parlour you can see out through the scullery (page 68), and down the garden path. The boldly chamfered spine beam, with its run-out stops, implies that the building is late 16th or early 17th century. However, enthusiasts should beware the temptation of such rules of thumb when seeking a date.

began. Whitewash (ground chalk, water and size) and limewash, made from slaked quicklime with a binder of rock alum or tallow, were obviously the cheapest and most widely used interior finishes. Oil paints were in use in the Middle Ages, but were certainly not employed by poor cottagers until the eighteenth century. However, it is quite possible that in better cottages, owned or inhabited by more prosperous people, woodwork was oil painted in the seventeenth century.

Most people's idea of a cottage interior is Victorian in origin and at that time paint would have been normal, as would stencilled decoration (by then going out of fashion), wallpaper, and the lugubrious staining and graining which one associates with station waiting rooms and public libraries. The general rule must be – the earlier the cottage, the more stark and simply decorated it would be.

Expressions like 'hearth and home' and 'returning to his own hearth' precisely state the basic centre of cottage life. The fire was the most important factor in what was frequently a fight for survival. It provided warmth, it was used for all the cooking and it was a principal source of light. Although cottage folk went to bed early and rose at dawn, most of them could scarcely afford to turn in at five o'clock of a winter evening for they still had work to do. Cottage industry might include spinning, weaving, basket-making, candle- and rushlight-making, as well as lace-making. These and a host of other occupations could bring in additional income. Often they were the only means of earning a living.

The central bonfire in open-hall cottages would have fire dogs upon which to lean the burning logs, thus encouraging air for combustion. Bread was baked on a girdle and baking iron. Cooking pots either rested on the coals or were suspended from iron tripods. Cottages with genuine fireplaces could be expected to have simple stone or plaster hoods on corbels with wide tapering flues rising to chimneys poking out of the thatch. In the more opulent cottages the fireplace was set into a broad projecting chimney breast or, when the chimney breast was external, the lintel might run flush with the wall.

By the seventeenth century, many cottages had bread ovens built into the back or side wall of the fireplace. They had iron doors and were of vaulted construction in stone or brickwork. At the end of the century clay or 'cloam' ovens were being manufactured, which simplified the whole business and made it relatively easy to insert an oven in a fireplace which formerly had none.

The 'down-hearth' method of cooking straight onto the fire continued but there were more aids to roasting and boiling water. Spit-dogs, which acted as cradles for long iron roasting spits, were often used, and chimney cranes allowed the cooking pots to be swung over the fire. Some had three actions – swivel, vertical and horizontal. Iron kettles were extremely heavy and a tilting mechanism called an 'idle-back' was hung from the crane or chimney pothook so that you could tilt the kettle without removing it.

The eighteenth century was the age of the pattern book and the nineteenth continued the trend. The landed gentry, inquiring, imitative and sometimes altruistic, became zealous to improve the conditions of their work people. They not only did much to foster better and more practical housing, but turned their attentions to new designs for all manner of fixtures and fittings. No book on cottages can avoid mentioning the works of J. C. Loudon, a prodigiously energetic and inventive Scotsman, whose *Encyclopaedia of Cottage, Farm and Villa Architecture and Furniture* of 1833 became an essential guide. He covered everything from Italianate lodges to farm drains, bell pulls, shelf brackets, ottomans and four-poster beds. In my edition of 1842, he devotes nine pages to cottage stoves, ovens and fireplaces.

By this date the use of ranges (first devised in the 1780s) was becoming widespread. 'When the cottager can afford to purchase a range having an oven on one side and a boiler on the other, the kind which we consider the most suitable is that first made by Mr. Eckstein of London,' says he. It could be bought retail for five guineas. Basically, there were two types of range – the open and closed patterns. The former had cast-iron flat hobs over the oven and boiler but an open fire in the middle. The closed ones, like the Cornish range, had a slab top to the fire as well, and the smoke was channelled back into a flue. Ranges were made by local foundries all over the country in all kinds of designs, but the Carron and Coalbrookdale companies were two of the most famous.

The main form of cottage lighting was the rushlight, made by dipping rushes in animal fat melted over the fire. These were burned in special rushlight holders with pincer jaws which allowed them to be held at an angle, since they would not keep alight when placed upright like a candle. Candles, made of beeswax or tallow, were also widely used, but were more expensive – partly because of a tax imposed in 1709 which was not repealed until 1831. Many improvements in the manufacture of candles took place in the first half of the nineteenth century culminating in the invention of paraffin wax, obtained from mineral oils. By the 1870s, the production of cheap paraffin oil lamps made it possible for the poorest cottagers to use that vastly more economical and effective form of lighting.

It is odd to think that in modern times, with the almost universal ownership of refrigerators and freezers, we have become well nigh paranoiac about the very real dangers of hidden germs from the supermarket. Like the cottager of 1850, the majority of people in 1950 did not have fridges and depended on a cool larder, in which various leftovers languished under fly covers, interesting green moulds being scraped off with a knife. These unhygienic practices did not appear to do us much harm, unlike the deadly viruses which lurk in chilled and frozen food today.

Many cottages still have larders or dairies, often placed in a lean-to or outshut under a steep cat-slide roof. Often this remains the one part of an old building which still retains the atmosphere of a cottage as we remember it. The flagstone floor, the slate shelves for standing and cooling produce, and that poignant and evocative smell of sour milk and damp whitewash recall the innocent simplicity of childhood. You remember the encompassing feather bed, the sound of apples thudding to the ground on a still September night, sloping ceilings and camphor-smelling cupboards lined with peeling, rose-sprigged paper. The vision is largely the product of the Victorian and Edwardian eras and the quintessential cottage bedroom is still like that.

The reality was in many cases rather different. In one cottage in Cornwall I was shown a tiny windowless cubicle onto a passage where the owner's three brothers slept, their sole source of daylight and ventilation being a little hinged hatch in the plank door. There were no pretty patchwork quilts and rose-scented evenings for them.

The very idea of a bedroom, as such, was foreign to all but the most prosperous citizens throughout most of the Middle Ages, when many of the occupants of the average manor house would doss down on the floor of the great hall. Later primitive one-room cottages might have built-in cupboard beds along one wall. Parents in two-bedroom buildings often had a room to themselves, the children being relegated to the other sleeping chamber; but no rule can be given for the distribution of sleeping space, since it was governed by the number in the family, the balance between sexes and the degree of segregation thought necessary. Older girls might be in service at nearby farms, boys could be housed with neighbours who had surplus accommodation or be apprenticed to tradesmen – like the young Oliver Twist, whose bed was a flock mattress under the counter of his master's coffin shop.

In the eighteenth century, references are frequently made to the truckle bed which was pulled out from under the four-poster; and relatively well-to-do travellers sharing a room in an inn sometimes found it necessary to share the bed with a stranger. Cottagers must have resorted to similar devices, employing sacks filled with straw and other materials for mattresses. Curtains were used to divide rooms at night and coats were called into service as blankets.

In 1760, Casanova, visiting a beautiful nun in the garret of a cottage (albeit in Savoy), describes how 'The peasant woman had put a long sack filled with straw against the wall; it served us as a seat, and a bottle on the floor served as the candlestick for the candle which gave us light.' There is no reason to believe that England would have provided much better in a labourer's cottage.

The peasant's few pieces of furniture, as records show, might amount to a crude settle,

NORFOLK

The outside privy provided the main means of sanitation in country areas until quite recent times. This one has a relatively recent galvanized bucket. You just dug a hole in the ground and emptied the bucket into that. Indeed a privy place, this is ideally suited to those of contemplative disposition – green foliage dripping with summer rain may be seen through the wide ventilation gap above the door, and blackbirds sing in the orchard. (See also pages 104–7.)

a table, a chair and a couple of three-legged stools, which would adjust themselves to the uneven surface of the kitchen floor. A simple ventilated cupboard fixed to the wall, out of the way of marauding rats and mice, housed the family's meagre rations, and rushlights or candles were kept in a box hung on nails above the fireplace lintel.

It was not until the Victorian era, particularly in towns, that those musty and under-used parlours with their antimacassars, brass-topped tripod tables, bulbous mahogany and blowsy but dispiriting sideboards, with backs of bevelled glass, became common-place. However, many cottages in the eighteenth and nineteenth centuries were occupied by people of vastly more substantial means than farm labourers or urban workers. The spinster sister of the prosperous merchant, the young curate, or the industrious self-employed craftsman or tradesman could all be found living in cottages of varying degree. Their furniture and equipment might be comparatively plentiful and elaborate.

The conditions of rural cottage folk were so taken for granted that few writers took the trouble to describe them in any detail. Even a benevolent Norfolk clergyman like Parson Woodforde, who clearly carried out regular acts of charity for his poor parishioners, devotes infinitely more space in his diaries to describing the gargantuan meals which he regularly consumed than to recording the cottage way of life. In 1788, for example, he says: 'I took a walk to a cottage just by Mr. Bodhams to see one Mary Brand an Old Woman of 80 who belongs to Weston... I found her spinning by the fire tho' she almost is blind. I gave her to buy Tobacco as she smokes 1 shilling.'

After shelter and warmth, the most important basic requirement was water. Some cottages had no form of water supply and it had to be carried in buckets or earthenware pitchers from the village pump. Many cottages had their own wells, which, provided they were not polluted by leaking drainpipes, privies, or cesspits, afforded a more healthy and reliable source of fresh water than the dubious piped system eventually introduced in many towns. Freshwater springs were commonly used, as were streams and rivers. Typhus and other hygiene-related diseases were an everyday hazard of cottage life and could wipe out entire families in the space of a few months.

Nearly every cottage had its garden and Fanny Burney's husband, M. d'Arblay, dreamed of having 'cabbage walks - potatoe Beds - Bean perfumes and peas blossoms'. He was to have a flower garden as well; but this was not typical of a real cottage garden, where any flowers would have been grown in among the vegetables. At the end of the garden the prudent householder set up a timber privy. This could be a proper earth closet, with a seat over a bucket, which was filled periodically with earth and then emptied. Less encouraging was the practice of moving the privy so that the seat was positioned over a succession of new holes in the ground. In a stiff clay soil the effect of this procedure was to create a confusion of half emptied mini-cesspits. The most popular means of soil disposal in primitive cottages was to throw the contents of the chamber pot on the garden or let it heap up against the very walls of the hovel.

Not long ago one could still see cottage folk emptying the chamber pot on the vegetable garden and sometimes on the cinder path which ran down the middle. The brave new world of cars and coach lamps is very recent in the scale of things. As a boy during the war, I vividly recall seeing an old shawl-woman smoking a clay pipe on her front doorstep in a Shropshire town. Indeed, you do not have to be a 'greybeard loon' to bore the young with: 'I remember when it was all green fields.'

While cottage exteriors may retain most of the distinctive features which denote their age, style and regional materials, the interiors have normally undergone far greater changes. In fourteen months spent tracking down cottages for this book, the main objective has been to discover buildings which hint at that original simplicity which everybody finds so appealing but which is so difficult to preserve. The loveliest cottages are those where the least radical alterations have occurred; but for most owners there is no escaping the amenities of modern living, nor would they wish to forgo the solace of adequate heating, plumbing, lighting and kitchen gadgetry. In the last event, much of the charm of cottage interiors is dependent upon what goes into them in terms of books and furniture, rugs, pictures, china, brass and fabrics. The cottage of 1790 would have had little to please the eye, although the cottager's few possessions would doubtless have had the merit of not seeming synthetic by our standards.

The clever and imaginative cottage owner can usually retain that all too elusive sense of age, without being forced to adopt the primitive discomforts endured by the original inhabitants. No need perhaps to read Anita Brookner by rushlight or dash through the frost-laden garden to the privy at bedtime. Why bring away cobwebs and flaking whitewash with a feather duster, when matt emulsion paint provides almost the same agreeable austerity and visual calm?

The quest for the unspoiled cottage has been by turns diverting, frustrating, instructive, lonely, and, just when your heart was in your boots, could offer some hauntingly beautiful reward. In the early November dusk of some benighted and distant dale, when it became clear that you would be better occupied in writing the definitive guide to the English toasted sandwich, a benign deity might provide a felicitous discovery. At the edge of a secret and sleepy hamlet, where cottage life was once the reality and inheritance, rather than a dream, you might enter the cottage of cottages. There, despite alterations and the passage of time, would be revealed all those poignant reminders of past generations, whose home it used to be.

CORNWALL

The rural simplicity of this former cottage kitchen in West Cornwall abounds in interest but gives little clue to its date. The cast-iron range by H. Curnow is late 19th century and the 'medieval' arch was formed by the present tenants, using a salvaged 19th-century Gothic door from a nearby building. The child's chair, in the manner of 18th-century country Chippendale, the Caucasian rug and library globe of 1823, imply a degree of sophistication; less so, the Staffordshire and Mason's Ironstone on the chimney shelf. The building is in fact late 18th century, has a thatched roof and lies deep in the woods of an estate. The life tenants took it on when it was in a derelict condition and had been officially condemned.

Little staircase windows in thick cob walls are tailor-made for displaying glass. A selection of 19th-century medicine bottles with four modern goblets and an oil lamp with a glass reservoir adopt an almost human relationship, like figures in an opera frozen in some dramatic impasse. Less romantically, they were dug up from the garden. Of necessity gardens were habitually used for interring the rubbish of daily life and few owners will not have dug a fork into hidden tobacco tins and bed springs.

The search for additional space brought about this effective embrasure. The back partition wall was knocked through into the buttery outshut and the floor loads picked up by a beam resting on two granite columns – not salvaged from some 17th-century loggia, but agricultural field rollers stood on end. Such liberties may puzzle future historians, but only a heartless pedant would count this as other than a success story. The manager of a working granite quarry in the area estimated four or five days of hammer and chisel work was needed to convert a rectangular block of stone into a 5-foot-long roller.

Additional light for this bedroom was obtained by knocking a window through the flue leading from the range in the room below. Interestingly, this very wide flue had projecting stones inside it which could have been footholds for a chimney sweep's boy to ascend while cleaning. The two oak chairs are probably late 17th century, although some changes have been made to the caned seats. 'God speed the plough', reads the lustre cider mug on the broad window ledge.

CORNWALL

This tiny cottage parlour near Camelford shows how much can be made from a little white box of a room by filling it with objects which please the eye. The 18th-century practice of hanging many pictures in a relatively haphazard fashion is wonderfully vindicated by this assortment of topographical prints, watercolours and portraits in oil. Originally you would have stepped straight through the front door into the room, but an inner porch has been formed by constructing a partition on the left.

The parlour leads through a matchboard partition to the second and only other ground-floor room, which is the kitchen. This also accommodates a staircase with a pole handrail, square balusters in the Regency manner and a turned newel post with an acorn finial which is unmistakably late Victorian or Edwardian in design. Such newel posts were turned out in their tens of thousands to embellish the stairs of those endless rows of urban terraced houses at the apogee of Empire.

CORNWALL

The bedroom over the parlour of the little cottage near Camelford, despite the plethora of books and pictures, is really furnished almost as minimally as it would have been when it housed a labourer. A brass bedstead, a stool and a chest of drawers is all he could have afforded; and all anybody could manage to fit into the space to this day.

Cottage-dwellers these days usually feel the need for one decent-sized room, so cottages tend to lose their downstairs partitions. This pair of former miners' cottages in the granite uplands near Redruth is a case in point. The robust and satisfying Cornish range would have dominated a small square room. Now, the whitened joists, heavy carved oak Victorian settle and sideboard and the red plush table cover combine to invoke the cool tranquillity of a 17th-century Dutch interior. This small granite building most likely dates from the first quarter of the 19th century.

The other end of the room dispels any notions of Vermeer or de Hoogh. The big granite down-hearth is as Cornish as could be. Most log fires have their own peculiarities. This one demands that it be lit to one side so the smoke will find its way up the commodious but off-centre flue above. The fact that it will burn huge, unsplit rounds of timber without smoking surprises anyone who has had much to do with repairing and restoring old hearths. The exposed stonework of the chimney breast is not a feature you would have seen in the 19th century. It would have been plastered or whitewashed over – indeed some plaster can still be seen clinging to the left-hand end of the huge lintel.

The kitchen of the same cottage boasts another Cornish cast-iron range. This one is of Redruth manufacture and is late 19th century. It is in working order and has been adapted to heat water as well. The glazed earthenware sink, brass bib taps and wooden draining board all accord with the satisfying sense of texture and substance which the cottage proclaims.

CORNWALL

CORNWALL

The owners of this upland croft cottage in far West Cornwall found it an abandoned wreck. The roof slates had cracked and crumbled, rafters, floors and inner lintels had rotted away. This room and the one above it were all that remained of the original early-18th-century building to which had been added a rather dull and symmetrical cottage in about 1860. For many years the part seen in the picture was used for farm purposes, but when the place was restored, new floorboards, joists, sash windows and doors were fitted. Now a hall and dining room, the floor is not of flagstones as you might suppose, but made of concrete slabs finished with wax polish. The big carving dish on the mahogany Sutherland table by the door, is Spode 'Landscape' pattern.

The main room in the Cornish miner's croft, looking from the fireplace end towards the hall, which is glimpsed through the open ledged-and-braced door. The latter is seen to be modern from its relatively narrow boards. 'Books do furnish a room' was the cliché from which Bagshaw, in Anthony Powell's splendid novel, derived his nickname. It is now scarcely possible to avoid recalling that banal dictum when faced with a wall of volumes, stacked from floor to ceiling. The view here suggests that furniture, bit and bobs of glass, pictures and ornaments also play their part. The reading stand, *c.* 1830, folds down to make a chair. Although this room looks large, it is really of quite modest proportions.

The 1860s part of the upland croft was probably the home of a miner, who also farmed the few acres around the building. The central window was once the front door, leading into a narrow passage with a small square room on either side. The fireplace has been converted into a big log-burning hearth, but must have been built to contain a Cornish range. As cottages go, this one is furnished with a good deal of sophistication. The furniture has clearly started out in a much grander house than this one. However, the simple white plastered walls, wool curtains, and open-joisted ceiling with exposed boards, recall the building's lowly status.

CORNWALL

In the summer of 1743, Elizabeth, wife of Digory Isbell, a journeyman stonemason, gave refreshments to two strangers who were travelling the lonely road from Launceston to Bodmin. They insisted on paying her for her hospitality and then knelt to pray 'without a book'. They were John Nelson and John Downes, advance agents for the preacher John Wesley. A year later Wesley himself was entertained in the little four-square house at Trewint, beside what is now the A30. Digory Isbell resolved to form a Methodist Society there and it flourished until the spate of chapel building made it redundant. Finally, it became a ruin; but in 1950 it was restored and is now thought to be the smallest Methodist preaching place in the world. You open a door into a narrow flagstoned passage, at the end of which this tiny white-walled room remains open to receive the faithful.

CORNWALL

When present-day cottage owners start to strip the paper off old walls, the colours and textures thus revealed seem to provide an irresistible temptation to call a halt to the process of redecoration. 'Like a faded fresco', the artist owner explained. The changes have been rung to some extent by the use of subtly stencilled leaf motifs, which give the impression that they were there in the first place. The granite building is early 19th century but the twelve-pane sash windows with projecting horns on the stiles are modern copies. The right-hand windowsill has a tiller embellishment of brass dolphins from the captain's gig of H.M.S. *Tamar*. Bertie, the King Charles Spaniel, poses with calm scepticism.

One of the principal charms of old cottages with thick stone walls is the depth of door and window openings. The wide splays on either side of the sash help to distribute more light into the room – a point which those adding extensions to such houses would do well to remember, otherwise absence of wall depth is infinitely noticeable when you step from the old into the new. This window is in the rear wall of the cottage, which, like so many, has had an intervening partition removed to turn two rooms into one. The owner's paintings hang on the splays. The Victorian fringed pelmet is cut from a 14-foot roll of cotton twill embroidered in petit point. A blue-and-white Spode footbath filled with heather forms the centrepiece of the sill arrangement.

CORNWALL

The whitewashed fisherman's cottage stands a few feet above the lane. At dusk, the lighted interior conveys a sense of mystery and welcome which teases the memory and invites speculation. Other open doors in other villages, long ago, are brought to mind and then dispelled by the fleeting impact of this new discovery. What is it really like inside? You can see the answer on page 2.

DEVON

The clue to the age of this cottage near Tiverton is the beautiful oak muntin-and plank partition wall in the sitting room. It is load bearing and divides the room from the former dairy of what used to be a small two-up and two-down 16th-century farm, onto which a single bay was added in the 18th century. The horizontal window opening would once have contained a timber-framed mullioned window – there is still one of these in existence. The floor has been relaid by the present owners, using Welsh roofing slates. The chair is of beechwood with a dished elm seat. It is a Victorian forerunner of the typist's swivel.

DEVON

The roof construction of the Devonshire farmhouse can be seen in this picture. The curved cruck timber rises out of the wall (in the right-hand corner) and is mortice-and-tenon jointed into the principal rafter which lies on top of it. These roof timbers have been repaired, so the cruck is dowelled rather than peg jointed to a new length of rafter, neatly scarfed to the original one. The wall plaster, laid on wattle and daub, has been painted with limewash given its seductive colour by the addition of ochre pigments. The Victorian brass bed came from a nearby farm and the patchwork quilt was made by the lady of the house.

The staircase is housed in a small projection beneath the main roof slope. Movement of the purlin, which runs horizontally above the stairhead, seems to have pulled the flimsy stud partition outwards. The purlin bears the irregular toothmarks of a pitsaw. Another repaired cruck and principal rafter can be seen by the door. The pine floorboards have been refinished, and a Turkey runner covers the landing passage.

DEVON

DEVON

Born and bred in the rural heartlands which lie between Dartmoor and Exmoor, this Devon farmer still keeps proudly to the timeless routines which govern the lives of those who work the land. His cottage has a 19th-century flavour, but jointed-cruck roof timbers (not seen here) suggest an earlier date. Logs are burned on the Esse stove which makes this little parlour snug on cold winter evenings.

A farmer who still keeps pedigree Jersey cattle must not dismiss the Ministry of Agriculture circulars lightly, even if they have a way of monopolizing desk space. This Victorian sideboard seems ideally suited to its purpose. It stands in the through passage between the parlour of a Devon cottage and the kitchen, with its lath back chairs and 19th-century table.

WILTSHIRE

WILTSHIRE

The inexorable charm of limestone flags is the making of this cottage room. Many people treasure them, but it is a shocking fact that modernizers often ruthlessly screed flags over to provide a nice even surface for carpet and other contemporary finishes. Once covered with hard cement-based mortar they are usually beyond reclamation. 'Grip' floors, made of beaten lime and ashes, were often used in cottages, but prove impracticable today.

WILTSHIRE

The most pleasing and adaptable sink you can put in an old cottage is the glazed earthenware trough which takes its name from Belfast. Hardwood draining boards, so despised in the flabby fifties and swinging sixties, are now decidedly chic. Until the post-war years nobody had anything else, whether the boards tilted into a copper-lined sink in the scullery of a great house, or into a stone sink in the back kitchen of a farm or cottage. The mullioned window with its bold ovolo mouldings could well be 17th century, but originally would have been lead glazed.

WILTSHIRE

Who would guess that the wall in which this door is set is part of the original fabric of a rubble-stone Cotswold long-house of the late 14th century. The building would have been single storey with a thatched roof, hall, cross-passage and shippon. The height was raised to make a one-and-a-half storey house in the 17th century, and was finally roofed with Cotswold stone 'tiles' in the 18th century, when the lean-to kitchen was added. A gin trap hangs behind the door and on the dresser is a collection of 18th-century Coalport and early-19th-century Miles Mason china.

The former Cotswold long-house has an early-19th-century fitted pine dresser, with flush-beaded vertical boarding. On the upper shelves is a late-Victorian dinner service. The elm armchair with ring-turned legs and arm uprights is probably *c.* 1840. The little eight-pane sash window in the room beyond is of late-Georgian pattern, without cords or weights. You prop it open with a stick.

WILTSHIRE

Not quite a cottage, but who could resist this 17th-century oak panelling. Scratch-moulded muntins and rails of this kind can be seen in the construction of oak chests, court cupboards and doors throughout the Stuart period. The marquetry chest-on-stand is also 17th century, with typical cross-stretchers bracing barleysugar-twist legs – a popular Baroque design. The heavy steel door hinges and keyhole escutcheon are surprisingly crude in this context.

The fireplace is of considerable interest because it embodies many of the classical motifs which were favoured in early English Renaissance buildings. It probably dates from the mid-17th century. By this time classical disciplines were much better understood, but such practices as putting scoop mouldings in the frieze were throwbacks to Jacobean naivety. The original fireplace opening has been outlined with a guilloche moulding of interlacing circles. The centre has been filled in to accommodate a smaller grate, in place of the big down-hearth and firedogs.

HAMPSHIRE

Not far from Bedales School in Hampshire are a number of small buildings inspired by the Arts and Crafts Movement. Sydney Barnsley rented this building for his son Edward Barnsley from a rich Bedalian called Geoffrey Lupton. He subsequently bought it in 1925. The cottage was built by Lupton in 1908. Both Sydney and Edward were inventive furniture-makers and designers, and much of the furniture in the building was made by either father or son.

HAMPSHIRE

Edward Thomas the poet worked here. The room was built for him just before the Great War, in which he died. His benefactor was the builder Geoffrey Lupton, who was educated at nearby Bedales. Through the more recent opening, to the left of the fireplace, and under the same roof, is the part Lupton constructed as a shed to store beekeeping equipment. This simple room provided a private place for the poet, who lived in various houses nearby. Both Robert Frost and Rupert Brooke are said to have visited him in his sanctum. The books and furniture belong to the present owner.

SURREY

SURREY

Oakhurst Cottage at Hambledon in Surrey is a former labourer's cottage owned and opened to the public by the National Trust. Its timber framing suggests a 17th-century or early-18th-century date. The Trust have furnished it with country items from a collection made by Gertrude Jekyll (1843–1932), who lived nearby. Miss Jekyll was a dedicated gardener who drew inspiration from the informal and traditional cottage style. She laid out numerous gardens for country houses, some of her best being designed in collaboration with the original and inventive architect Edwin Lutyens. From 1900 to the 1930s Oakhurst Cottage, it is said, was home to a family which comprised father, mother, eight children and a lodger.

'The joy of the Lord is your strength' declares the embroidery hanging on the boarded partition at the top of the stairs in Oakhurst Cottage. Wherever it came from, it is wholly representative of the morally uplifting quotations which cottage folk displayed in the 19th century to proclaim the faith and fortify the morale. The charming asceticism of rooms with broad polished boards and minimal furniture is frequently abandoned by modern cottage dwellers in favour of fitted carpets and built-in wardrobes. The less sybaritic approach is frequently a sign that the owners do not live there all year round.

A triumph of equipoise, the kettle is suspended from an 'idle-back' or 'lazy-back' tilter with an elegant serpentine handle. This gadget, often 18th century, made it unnecessary to lift heavy, hot and smoke-blackened kettles when pouring boiling water. As in this case, the idle-back was usually hung on a ratchet pothook which could be adjusted to allow the kettle or cauldron to be raised and lowered over the flames. The pothook, in its turn, was attached to an iron bar set from front to back of the flue.

The wash-house of Oakhurst Cottage is a far cry from the modern utility room, although it served the same purpose for generations of occupants. Clearly, washing for a large family in a small house was an important function, and it was afforded a good deal of valuable space. However, this room also served for baking and the built-in oven, on the left, has a corbelled hood which recalls the design of the great open fireplaces seen in early medieval buildings. The splendid sink, hollowed out of a single block of stone, is the kind that nowadays is more often seen planted out with geraniums.

SURREY

When this was built in the 1860s, brick cottages put up to house farm labourers who worked the rich land of the Thames Valley demonstrated a relatively new sense of *noblesse oblige* on the part of the landed gentry. Twenty miles away were the fetid slums so graphically described in Henry Mayhew's *London Labour and the London Poor*. Conditions here, while spartan and probably overcrowded, constituted a major improvement. Now the minuscule kitchen and parlour are knocked into one living room, which must astonish the ghosts of the former inhabitants, although some of the furniture should strike a familiar note.

SURREY

The innocent confusion of this cottage kitchen gives no hint of its antique origins. In fact, it is the early-16th-century nucleus of a minuscule one-and-a-half-storey cottage which contains a rare timber-framed smoke bay. The blackened timber and plaster of the bay can still be seen by lifting a hatch in the ceiling. Smoke bays predate the introduction of brick or stone hearths and stacks and often, like this one, let the smoke out through an open gablet at the peak of the roof. The mellow floor of brick (sometimes called 'pavoirs') is typical of the area.

An early-19th-century mirror in the larger 18th-century addition to the cottage reflects an array of Italian maiolica in its smoky silvered glass. The wall stencilling was done by the owner and friends in the 1970s. The curtains are Transylvanian, woven from hemp-fibre yarns and band-block printed with indigo pigment.

Although it has a cottage flavour, the early-18th-century addition to a tiny timber-framed building is really a small house. The sitting room has exposed joists and a chamfered and stopped spine beam. The joists have been painted with some more of the Swedish-inspired motifs seen on the walls. The decorative painting of beams continued in Europe long after it had been abandoned in England. English houses, which might have had painted timbers in medieval times, tended to have beams left in their natural state during much of the 17th century. Once Renaissance influences caught on, joists were normally ceiled over with lath and plaster. Beams too were plastered and embellished with a continuation of the cornice mouldings. On the wall above the George II sideboard hangs a Gujarat bridal decoration from Northern India, fringed with pennants which represent local villages.

SURREY

This interesting late-17th-century or early-18th-century pine dresser is open at the bottom. The vase-shaped splat in the middle has a similar design to those used for the backs of chairs and for staircase balusters at that period. The fretted bow of the drawer rail links the central splat with a half-vase respond. This bow or ogee design was often used as a decorative form of door head, especially in Monmouthshire farmhouses. The cottage is owned by a potter, and here we see her collection of European slipware. The wall painting on the right is a modern version of naive Swedish themes.

The fireplace is placed in the back wall of the house, perhaps because the tiny medieval building to which this part is attached made it more difficult to insert the more usual gable stack. Brick walls have been constructed within the hearth to restrict its width and better channel the smoke into the flue.

WEST SUSSEX

Few people are prepared to use the roof space in an old building without making major changes to its structure if tie beams and collars get in the way. The owner of this cottage has shown commendable restraint. It must be agreeable for enthusiasts to lie in bed and trace the components of this 18th-century roof with its original principal rafters, pegged common rafters, butt purlins, struts, and collars. The most inconvenient tie is the one just below and behind the dangling net floats, which have been draped over an improvised collar bolted to a pair of common rafters. The proper tie beam was obviously cut away at some stage to allow people to move around in the roof space, and struts were used to link the roof timbers with the beam under the floor. However, this measure was clearly found to be inadequate and the replacement tie subsequently put in.

This was once the village bakehouse. Mr Mills, the baker, came up from nearby Easebourne once or twice a week to produce the bread which the present tenant's parents sold in their cottage shop next door. For the last seventy years or so the building has been used as the family's coalshed and store. The wavy brick floor is typical of Sussex. Wherever you go in the Midhurst area, you will see the distinctive yellow paint on doors and windows of properties which form part of the Cowdray estate.

The great open hearth of the village bakehouse, near Easebourne, suggests that the building might once have been a dwelling. The ovens were reached by an opening on the left (not visible in the picture), and they protruded from the back wall under their own roof. Coal cascades through the open door of what used to be a storeroom.

WEST SUSSEX

Not exactly your idea of a cottage, perhaps, but that is exactly what it used to be. This tall, cool, Victorian dairy, near the Cowdray ruins at Midhurst, was converted from estate workers' dwellings, hence the high windows which would have lighted their upper storeys. The private dairy of a great house often included a fountain and basin set in the tiled floor to keep the temperature down. Blue-and-white tiles, assembled to form suitably pastoral scenes, were particularly popular in the 1880s and '90s. A wooden butter churn and scales stand on the broad marble ledge.

WEST SUSSEX

From this beam, in the scullery of a timber-framed estate worker's cottage, would hang the newly killed pig. Afterwards, the uneven brick floor was sluiced down and the water drained out of the door into the garden. Here, too, they washed the clothes in a copper and baked in an oven, now removed. Cowdray estate tenants' cottages do not have names but numbers. C74 has been the present occupant's home from childhood to the present day. He has worked for 46 years as gardener at a nearby private house.

WEST SUSSEX

This Sussex cottage retains the true flavour of country life as most people, who are old enough to do so, remember it. Flush-beaded boards line the walls. The haphazard plumbing arrangements – familiar to anyone who has owned old buildings, where the concealment of pipes presents a problem – recall the fact that any sort of hot-water system was a major achievement until quite recent times. The television set and its portable aerial will one day help some earnest researcher to date the scene.

WEST SUSSEX

What is the meaning of this Tudoresque affair? No species of vernacular building comes instantly to mind. Imagine a substantial 16th-century stone water tower, converted to domestic purposes towards the end of the 17th century. That settles the peculiar shape. Salvage the curious interior timberwork from a provincial branch of Boots the Chemists and this giddy amalgam of studs and rails and 'Queen Anne' newel posts is the comic but endearing result. It is now the home of the Curator of the Cowdray ruins at Midhurst.

KENT

KENT

In a woodland clearing near Cowden in Kent is a cottage which used to be a late medieval hall-house. This is, in fact, the remains of a cross-wing, which the Landmark Trust has turned into a holiday cottage. Since no student of architectural history could leave Kent without seeing a crown-post roof, here is a fine, if plain, example. The common rafters are tied together with collars, which rest upon a high collar purlin, running the length of the building. This, in turn, is supported at intervals by the crown posts themselves, which rise from the centres of heavy tie beams, arch braced at their junctions with the main wall posts.

KENT

The attic studio of a miniature painter monopolizes every inch of the space beneath the rafters of the half-hipped roof. A wide skylight illuminates her easel, at which she sits perched on high, rather like St Jerome at his desk in the National Gallery painting by Antonello da Messina. However, she has a better view and there are no lions padding out of the dark.

It is sometimes claimed that there is no art or poetry in plumbing – pragmatic plastics put the muse to flight. The idea that the man who fitted this pipework had been sitting up in bed at night leafing through colour plates of abstract paintings must be an intolerable flight of fancy. 'Dauntless' says the label on the cistern; and what could be more so than this essay on inflection.

KENT

Kent is a county rich in 'dream cottages', but more often than not the interiors have been so modernized and tarted up that they cease to claim one's affection from the moment the threshold is crossed. The sense of age conveyed by mellow tiled roofs and mullioned windows is eradicated once their owners begin to spend money on 'improvements'. This one, near Goudhurst, is the home of a talented miniature artist who has made a point of retaining the tiled floors, battered 17th-century doors and other original features.

What is that nebulous thing called 'atmosphere'? Do the walls of an old building record and replay the joys, miseries and dramas which punctuated the lives of its former inhabitants? Sitting in this cottage room in the half-light of an October afternoon, there is a sense of peace which lingers in the memory long after its architectural qualities have been forgotten.

KENT

This Kentish 'cottage' was originally constructed for the warden of a charity founded to provide work and accommodation for poor people in the area. The farmhouse, as it must have been, has seen various changes of status over the centuries. Money from the charity is still available to help girls of the parish to be married in church, free of charge; and to provide Christmas funds for the elderly. Above the Venus of Milo's head can be seen a blocked-up mullion window.

KENT

An attic staircase of perilous ingenuity, in the 16th-century charity warden's house, would set the teeth of any modern building control officer on edge. It would be too narrow, too steep and the 'going' from front to back of the winders is wonderfully inadequate. A curved tread gets you around the difficult corner.

KENT

Now an antique shop in the village of Biddenden, Kent, this cottage was once a bakery. The oven has been converted by the owners into a log-burning fireplace. Out of hours the back part of the building is used as a sitting room. Called 'The Two Maids', the name derives from the curious story of Elisa and Mary Chulkhurst, Siamese twins who were born nearby in 1100. When one died, the other, refusing separation, expired six hours later. They left money for the poor, and in their memory rolls impressed with a 'two maids' design are still handed out in the village on Easter Monday. The fire-dogs are dated 1677. The bellows are Georgian, the oak chair 17th century and the sampler on the wall was stitched by 10-year-old Jane Orford in 1817. Burmese Bluebell keeps the china dogs company.

KENT

Not everything on this side of the back room at The Two Maids antique shop is quite what it seems, although the lovely mellow brick floor on the right is genuine enough. The convincing plank door was, in fact, made by the owners, the joists are recent replacements and the handsome oak settle is thought to have been put together in Victorian times from pieces of early oak panelling. The barn owl in a case looks as though it might be planning to devour some small animal just out of sight – a Burmese kitten, perhaps.

LONDON

The sitting room of an artist, potter and gardener in North London expresses her love of colour, while also conveying a sense of casual ease. Widely travelled, the trophies of her wanderings fill this little 19th-century house – the end one of a typical terrace. The green stable door gives access to a conservatory. A golden and gorgeous curtain has been swagged back like some magnificent portière.

The terrace house was once a shop with a big window onto the street. There, beyond the book shelves, which form a partition, the owner works at her pottery. This little conservatory fills the tiny yard between the whitewashed brick wall on the left and the door to the kitchen on the right. Beyond, lies the garden. Biddy, a former resident of Battersea Dogs Home, turns her best side to the camera.

LONDON

LONDON

By the middle of the 19th-century, big cities like London were full of semidetached 'cottages', built for clerks and shopkeepers. This one of about 1840 has a small but relatively grand parlour, now decorated and furnished in the manner of the Aesthetic Movement of the 1870s and '80s. The wallpaper is reprinted from a design by J.H. Dearle who worked for Morris & Co. The fireplace is the plainest marble possible, with an 1880 grate. Its splays have Minton tiles. The curtains are antique early-Victorian chintz, hung on heavy brass poles in the form of arrows. On the mantel shelf are Parian figures, including Queen Victoria and Prince Albert. Above, is an engraving of Paddington Station after Frith, in its original oak frame.

The former breakfast room of the London semi was arched through to form a double drawing room around 1860. The ebonized chair in the background was designed or inspired by the architect E.W. Godwin, lover of Ellen Terry. On the right is an oak standing writing desk, probably designed by Bruce Talbert in about 1880. Talbert worked for the great Victorian-Gothic architect, George Edmund Street. The hanging corner bracket is by Henry W. Batley, who was Talbert's pupil. His *Series of Studies for Domestic Furniture and Decoration* (1883) shows that the clock is an optional extra.

LONDON

LONDON

Countless thousands of small houses and cottages, built to shelter the workers in the Great Wen, spread south of the River Thames. Legatees of this massive expansion must now find ways to counter the inevitable uniformity, like the owners of this Battersea cottage of *c.* 1800–30, who have resorted with considerable success to the device of subtle colours and forgiving contents. A sink, draining board, and cupboard made from salvaged pine soften an architecturally featureless kitchen. The rich brown 18th-century stick-back Windsor chairs, the slatted wooden sack carrier or hicking barrow above the sink and the diagonally scored wooden riddle (left of the window) all add texture and interest to the scene. Riddles, for spreading out the dough for oatcakes before baking, were commonly used in Scotland and the North of England.

Another corner of the kitchen in the Battersea cottage shows what can be done with an informal assortment of pottery and kitchen bygones. At the bottom of the wall display is a chopping or mincing knife. The heart-shaped object is a North-country peel used for moving oatcakes in and out of exceptionally hot beehive ovens. There is a late-19th-century rotary whisk, a truncheon-like stick, which could be a thible for stirring porridge, and a wooden-handled toasting fork. To its right is a rather primitive home-made skimmer – these were usually made from iron, brass or copper.

LONDON

The staircase in the same Battersea cottage is of the dog-leg variety, rising in a straight flight to the half-landing and doubling back to reach the first floor. It then repeats the operation but turns across the window by means of winders and a quarter-landing. The mahogany handrail and newel post are of a design much favoured in the first half of the 19th century. The staircase window is an eight-pane double-hung sash with thin glazing bars – a pattern which followed the multi-paned forms of the previous century.

Until quite recently, most people endured the stark, uniform and visually cheerless bathrooms which replaced those dignified and formidable affairs instituted in the Victorian and Edwardian eras. Mahogany-look bathrooms are now distinctly fashionable, but not always suited to cottage surroundings. This one has been fitted with pine dado panelling which has also been used to conceal the side of the modern bath. The taps and shower unit are brass. The laundry basket is encrusted with gesso flower decoration.

SUFFOLK

The sitting room of the Battersea cottage has the straight walls, smooth plaster and formal proportions of a more sophisticated building. Its relatively lowly status is made apparent by the lack of cornice mouldings, although these might be omitted or simplified on the upper floors of a house. Somebody has had fun painting the fireplace surround and decorating the frieze with naive topographical scenes, reminiscent of those seen in the main panel of early-18th-century continued chimneypieces in grand buildings. These were frequently the work of itinerant artists from the Low Countries. The oak joined stools are in the 17th-century manner with stretchers placed very low to the floor. The piece in the right foreground is a cobbler's bench upon which the craftsman sat astride while working.

The central chimney stack of a former Suffolk pub clearly served a hearth in this position, but the fireplace lintel has been renewed and the pine chimney shelf above, although on traditional ogee brackets, is a more recent innovation. Its supporting brickwork appears to have been restored but is in English bond, consisting of alternate rows of headers and stretchers. This bond went out of fashion in the 17th century. The delightful oak staircase is in a convincing position winding around the chimney stack but has been cleverly rebuilt. On the left of the door hangs an oak cupboard – not 1640 English as you might suppose, but Indian.

SUFFOLK

Formerly a Suffolk village inn, this 17th-century thatched and timber-framed building has been thoughtfully repaired and restored with the emphasis on retaining the texture of old oak and plaster. Commendably, the structural woodwork has not been coated with blackening gunge to give it the black-and-white look which some people imagine to be redolent of old world charm. In this case, there is a positively continental austerity seldom encountered in English houses and cottages. However, it gives a better impression of the severe surroundings in which most people lived before the 18th century. The fields behind the building were traditionally used for growing hemp for rope-making.

The converted village inn has 12-inch-wide oak floorboards. In general wide floorboards may be equated with age. Jointing methods varied, but in the 16th and 17th centuries it was usual for them to be rebated or just butted together instead of tongued and grooved. Sometimes there would be loose tongues which slotted into both adjoining boards. The external studwork of the walls contained wattle-and-daub panels which were usually limewashed over. The red paint on the plaster, a legacy from a previous owner, has been partially removed and left for decorative effect. A rag rug on the floor is a typical cottage feature. The painted cupboard, dated 1799, is East German and is considerably chocked up because of the steeply sloping floor.

SUFFOLK

Floored with East Anglian clay pamments – the purpose-made tiles of the area – the kitchen of the former Suffolk pub is the antithesis of 'modernization' and all that it has come to mean in connection with old buildings. This approach to the problem of retaining 'character' seems to be more frequently encountered in Norfolk and Suffolk than elsewhere in England. It is a technique which endears itself to artists and craftsmen who tend to possess a strong feeling for materials.

SUFFOLK

The village post office, while not entirely a thing of the past, has increasingly become a scaled-down version of a supermarket. The postmistress seen here at the counter of her Suffolk post office, spiritedly defends the comforting old-fashioned setting which has so long been her home and place of work. The cottage itself is probably 17th-century, with low ceilings and beams, but there is an early-19th-century bow window, inserted when it became a shop. Behind the Dickensian book-keeper's lectern from which she dispenses stamps and change are the drawers in which such necessities as mustard, caraway, ginger and starch were stored. 'Salt-petre' reads one of the labels, Gothic-lettered on gold leaf. Apart from being one of the ingredients of gunpowder, saltpetre was used for pickling meat, turning it a reddish colour in the process.

SUFFOLK

A bedroom in the Suffolk post office shows one of the principal rafters with a horizontal collar beam jointed into it. A diagonal brace between the two timbers appears to have been cut away to free some extra space. Braces in this position can be significant clues to medieval origins. The open door shows the traditional construction of vertical boards held together by flush-beaded ledges. The early-19th-century washstand has ring-turned mahogany legs and upon it is an elegant ewer, basin and covered soap dish. Underneath is an enamel slop pail into which basins and chamber pots were emptied.

The parlour of the post office cottage recalls with dream-like felicity the confident rural calm of an England before the First World War. One can hear the sound of Sunday bells and smell the roasting lamb, the cabbage and minty boiled potatoes from the garden. Who sang around that upright piano, 'Come into the Garden, Maude' and 'Gilbert the Filbert, the Colonel of the Nuts'? The bamboo display stand would have been particularly à la mode in the 1880s when the Japanese style was at its peak. 'I do *not* long for all one sees that's Japanese', sings Bunthorne in *Patience*.

The scullery in the post office cottage retains the pump with which water is still brought up from the well – the only form of supply. Lifting water to an overhead tank with a semi-rotary pump like this one can be a long, tedious and arm-aching business. Anyone who has lived or stayed in an isolated cottage may have experienced this least popular of chores, only rivalled by the somewhat alarming operation of lighting a Tilley lamp when experience is not on your side.

The wash-house was an essential adjunct to cottage domestic economy. The 'copper' was more often than not built into a corner, since this was both a convenient position for a circular cauldron and minimized the necessary brickwork. A fire was lit under the copper and the smoke escaped up a flue at the back. Not all 'coppers' were made of that material, some were cast-iron and those filled from hot-water taps could be zinc-coated or enamel. Most had to be filled by carting water in buckets from the pump or wellhead. The floor of this wash-house, although much cracked, is probably made of clay flooring tiles called pamments.

SUFFOLK

If you are looking for the much discussed rural simplicity of a really early building, this is it. The owners, with admirable respect for the history of vernacular architecture, have retained the undulating pamment-tiled floor of their late-15th-century cottage, and the crude door, made from three wide planks with an old Norfolk latch. Removing rugs and furniture gives some idea of what it might have been like five hundred years ago. The winding oak staircase was probably put in when the upstairs floor was inserted.

Late-medieval hall-houses often had unglazed mullioned windows of horizontal emphasis tucked up under the eaves. Upper floors like this one were constructed later, during the period sometimes referred to as 'The Great Rebuild' – the end of the 16th century and first half of the 17th century. Although they have suffered at some period from fairly severe beetle attack, the wide oak boards are of a quality which no sensitive owners would remove if they could possibly avoid doing so. The left-hand (gable) wall is of balloon- or box-frame design. The fifteen-pane fixed light with thin glazing bars seems to be early 19th century.

SUFFOLK

A sight which gladdens the heart of all old-building detectives – smoke-blackened roof timbers. The soot-encrusted rafters show that the building once had an open hall with a central hearth which sent the smoke curling up into the roof space. Even the riven battens appear to be original, although the thatch must have been replaced on a number of occasions. The brick chimney is probably a 17th-century insertion.

NORFOLK

Approached by a track which ends up in an orchard, this late-16th-to-early-17th-century farm labourer's cottage, not far from Fakenham in Norfolk, has been lovingly repaired by its present owner, with minimum disruption to its original features and materials. The tiny newel staircase has had some new elm treads and risers, and the plaster has been taken off the enclosing oak studwork to provide additional light. The old lath marks can still be seen on the timbers. The late-19th-century quarry tiles have been relaid on the floor and the brick partition wall unbuilt to provide a kitchen counter through to the living room. On the windowsill, the sculptural qualities of a 1970s Peugeot front axle differential give a new meaning to the term *objet trouvé*. The bench was salvaged from a Methodist chapel.

NORFOLK

At How Hill, near Potter Heigham, is the Environmental Centre for the Norfolk Broads. There they have repaired, furnished and opened to the public a gem of a tiny marshman's cottage. It is built of bricks made in a kiln nearby. Flints were used for the base of the walls as a crude form of damp-proof course. The marshmen earned their living trapping eels and shooting duck; they also cut reeds, sedge and marsh hay and looked after the windmills which powered the drainage pumps. A marshman called Ben Curtis was the last to live here and his speciality was catching eels in a net strung across the river. Although families might be large, this was the only downstairs room other than a larder. All the cooking was done on the rather minimal grate with its brick hobs to either side.

The upper floor of the marshman's cottage is reached by a winding staircase to the side of the hearth. Looking out through the bedroom door and across the landing is a gable casement window of Victorian pattern. A splendid patchwork quilt adds colour and interest to the iron bedstead, and the white enamel ewer and basin remind us of the less than luxurious conditions in which washing would have been attempted. No doubt on icy East Anglian winter mornings the water would have been frozen in the jug. A little cast-iron hoop grate let into the main chimney breast of the opposite gable wall could scarcely stay alight overnight. The probability is that this fire was seldom used except when a member of the family was ill. The wall mirror reflects the thin, flush-beaded matchboard ceiling, which slopes down almost to the floor.

NORFOLK

NORFOLK

Dairy Cottages, not far from Aylsham in Norfolk, form a group of attached buildings, the earliest being the remains of a 17th-century vicarage. This one is probably of slightly later date, but altered in the 19th century. It is built in Flemish bond brickwork and has a pantiled roof. You approach it by a cart track, the long summer grass brushing the engine casing of your car. The buildings are remote and beautiful fugitives from an age of cowslips and glow-worms and milk from the pail. Two cottages, each with a front door straight into the main room, have been knocked into one. Note the change in the floor tiles where the wall used to be.

Looking through from the kitchen at the back of the Dairy Cottage towards the front door, it is possible to see how people can capitalize on the texture of whitewashed brick walls and old tiled floors, without being obliged to furnish in an elaborate way. The cottage has an extremely active poltergeist, said to be the spirit of a young girl, which plucks mirrors from the wall and leaves them balanced upright on the floor. The owner apparently finds this presence more reassuring than frightening.

NORFOLK

There is a great deal to be said for having a bathroom – the exigencies of country life demand no less – though some might secretly think this one a trifle basic. It is situated in a brickbound slot between two of the Dairy Cottages and serves both houses, hence the additional tap, leading to a second hot-water boiler next door.

NORFOLK

This big open hearth is in another part of the Dairy Cottage grouping, sharing the tall slot of a bathroom with its neighbour. The big open fireplace was probably used for cooking in former times. It now contains an improvised brick box – a device many owners employ to improve the efficiency of their fires by confining them in a smaller area. Through the door to the right is a larder.

NORFOLK

The pantiled roof of an abandoned Norfolk woodman's cottage emerges between the sky and a bean field. Probably built in the mid-19th century, it is the single-storey forerunner of the ubiquitous bungalow. Victorian landowners, whether or not they followed his designs, were much influenced by J.C. Loudon's *Encyclopaedia of Cottage, Farm and Villa Architecture*, published in 1833. Many new houses for estate workers were built without an upper floor and demonstrated a great variety of styles, from Gothic to Italian Renaissance. This one has two rooms, a kitchen-wash-house and a small attached outbuilding.

The Norfolk woodman's cottage is a good example of a mid-19th-century estate worker's dwelling, which must have been counted a great innovation when it was built. This sad little abandoned kitchen-cum-wash-house does not lend itself to the cosy traditions of cottage life. One feels that it must have been very much a working kitchen. The lurid green paint on the brickwork of the sink, copper and fireplace is of recent vintage. It is interesting that a decent-quality hob grate of around 1850 has been fitted. The door above and to the right is for the oven.

NORFOLK

It is not thought good behaviour, but few readers will swear that they have never found the door of an abandoned cottage on the latch and sidled into the watchful gloom of empty rooms to satisfy their curiosity. When the author visited the Norfolk woodman's cottage, it was a rainy summer afternoon. Permission had been granted him, but the evidence of other intruders was not difficult to detect. Cigarette butts, soft-drink cans and crisp packets lay among the ashes of illicit fires. This tunnel-like window, with its view of the overgrown garden, provides a wistful reminder that someone had lived here not so very long ago, and bothered to string a net curtain across the cruciform glazing bars – more one suspects for decoration than privacy in this most remote of dwellings.

DURHAM

In the dales of Co. Durham, byre houses, where the cottage was perched on top of the stable or cattle byre, were still quite widely occupied until the beginning of this century. Access to the living space was reached by a flight of exterior steps. This one has been somewhat altered in height. There is evidence on the rear wall (not visible here) of almost defensively narrow window openings, reminiscent of Northumbrian fortified bastle-houses. The gable window suggests a sleeping loft reached by a ladder. The roof is of large sandstone flags – in this area often fixed with pegs made of sheep's rib bones. The window openings are of late-18th- or early-19th-century proportions and the windows themselves are modern copies of Victorian ones.

The cattle kept in the byre gave off sufficient warmth from their bodies to provide a form of central heating for the farmworker's living quarters above. The arched and chamfered sandstone door looks 17th century. Like the shippons (cattle sheds) of long-houses, the byre floor would slope with the land to drain at one end. This byre is still used for cattle and the rooms over are still employed as living accommodation. Livestock in humble farms were often stalled in close proximity to the inhabitants, sometimes sharing the ground floor with only a flimsy wooden partition in between.

Durham

A Victorian parlour in a miner's cottage. This convincing interior like those on the following pages is in one of a row of genuine cottages reconstructed at Beamish Open Air Museum, near Stanley. The buildings, which date from the 1860s, have been decorated and furnished in various styles with genuine furniture, pictures, papers and textiles. The fireplace has a typical cast-iron register grate with hoop-shaped opening. A printed velvet covering in the manner of an oriental rug has been placed on the table. The chairs are of the balloon-back pattern, much favoured during the middle third of the 19th century. Durham miners had a penchant for expensive furniture during the heyday of the Northeast coalfields in the 1890s. The American organ or harmonium symbolizes that relative prosperity. Singing *en famille* was a main form of self-entertainment in all classes of society.

Durham

The parlour window of the Beamish cottage has twelve panes divided by thin glazing bars in exactly the same design as you might see in an 18th-century building, except that the sash stiles have moulded horns which may be noticed protruding above the lace curtain on either side. The wallpaper is a modern reproduction of a mid-Victorian original. The window frame and sill are grained in the typical Victorian manner.

The kitchen of the same Beamish cottage centres on a fine open Newcastle brick range with a circular oven door – a distinctive feature in the Northeast. This type of range had an unusual water boiler, with an iron lining, which had to be filled and emptied by hand via a lid (in this picture it is behind the brickwork on the left). The steel fender provides a vital putting-down space for pots and pans hot off the fire. At each end are circular trivet plates, used here for standing flat irons. A vastly decorative brass drying rail is suspended from the mantel shelf upon which may be seen a Victorian steeple clock. What appears to be a substantial chiffonier is really a 'dess' bed – a cupboard concealing a fold-down iron or wooden bedframe. On its shelf are the familiar figures of Bonny Prince Charlie and Flora Macdonald, beloved of the Staffordshire potteries.

DURHAM

Additional bedroom space in cottages was always hard to come by. Secondary rooms were partitioned off in such a way that half the ceiling might be under the sloping rafters. This astonishing mahogany bed has turned and carved posts embellished with bun finials that are reminiscent of two Jacobethan stair newels linked with a rolling pin. Its somewhat phallic appearance is too funny to be intimidating. It has probably been cut down from a four-poster of about 1860.

One of the Beamish cottages is furnished in a 20th-century style, heavily influenced by the Art Deco fashion which lent itself so well to the new means of mass production. This Easiwork Kitchen Cabinet already displays the rather blandly functional qualities of the 1935–45 wartime Utility furniture. It is made of light oak and has a built-in enamel flour sifter, enamel pull-out top and roller-blind front. 'Delightful Dinner Menus for 3 Weeks', proclaims the notice inside the open cupboard door.

DURHAM

The Beamish Museum includes this 17th-century farmhouse, which has been completely rebuilt and furnished with total authenticity. The big kitchen with its flagstone floor has all the detail and atmosphere of a traditional working farmhouse from which the tenant has just stepped out to do the evening milking. The rag mats, rocking chair, huge settle, pewter plates and Yorkshire pattern range are infinitely beguiling. Originally, the big fireplace would have been used as a down-hearth, with meat, spit-roasted in front of the open fire. Cooking ranges like this one were normally fitted in the mid-19th century. Slung from the ceiling joists is a slatted 'flake' for cooling and drying oatbreads.

Nothing could speak more eloquently of cottage life than the larder in Beamish Museum's restored farmhouse. Certainly bigger and better equipped than in most cottages, its broad shelves on timber brackets and stone cooling slabs, supported by whitewashed bricks, suggest all the pattern, colour and texture which present-day cottage dwellers should be zealous to recreate. In the days when steel-bladed knives were commonplace, what more useful than Kent's Patent Rotary Disc Knife Cleaner of 1882?

DURHAM

CUMBRIA

The wash-house at the Beamish farm has a corner copper with its own grate to heat the water, and a big, shallow stone sink hollowed out of a single slab. A cone-shaped posser for dunking the washing is perched at the back of the copper and there is a washboard for rubbing stains. A drying horse is suspended from pulleys above the North-country open range. The latter is mid-19th century and has the typical oven with a circular door. The top bars of the grate are designed to fall forward forming a trivet for standing pots on.

Few Cumbrian cottages or farmhouses still retain quite such a mysterious and perfect example of a 17th-century newel staircase as this one near Ambleside. It is made from solid blocks of timber, each tread worn away in the middle by generations of former inhabitants. It is approached through a doorway in the splendid screen of moulded vertical planks at one end of the slate-flagged hall. Timber screens were used in most parts of England to partition the principal ground-floor room from the entrance door and cross-passage. Sometimes they were made from heavy timber studs with solid boards slotted into them, but not infrequently the entire screen was composed of boards, each rebated on one side to form a junction with its neighbour.

CUMBRIA

Dove Cottage at Grasmere was the home of the poet William Wordsworth and his sister, Dorothy, from 1799 to 1808. Formerly a tavern called The Dove and Olive Bough, 'this loved abode', as Wordsworth described it, entirely fulfilled their romantic fancies. The records of the Wordsworth Trust, who own the building and open it to the public, depict a fairly spartan existence, although by no means that of a deprived cottager. The panelling suggests the early 18th century, and the fitted drawers and cupboards to either side of the hearth are typical of the area. The fitted hob grate with its decorated cast-iron front plates is clearly late 18th or early 19th century. The cruciform-mullioned window is a diamond-paned pastiche of an earlier type of lead-glazed window seen in the late 17th century.

The kitchen at Dove Cottage has a fine mid-19th-century range of a North-country pattern similar to the Albert Kitchener range, with a central roasting fire, oven (top right) and water boiler under the left-hand hob. The lead-lined timber sink is a wonderfully satisfying affair and the fixed-light window with a single opening pane employs a form of minimal ventilation often encountered in early-19th-century bow and bay windows. A candle or rushlight box hangs on the wall to the right of the fire and there is a rushlight holder on the right of the chimney shelf.

CUMBRIA

Spice cupboards are a special feature in Cumbrian buildings. They were often built into the wall alongside the hearth, probably in the hope that they might be kept dry by the heat from the fire. Their contents of herbs, spices and possibly tea and sugar, were expensive commodities in the 17th and 18th centuries, hence the lock on the door. This cupboard is entirely typical with its carved initials and date. The scratch-moulded framing was commonly used for oak chests, court cupboards and dressers at this time, as were nailed butterfly hinges.

SHROPSHIRE

The open hearth of a late-16th-to-early-17th-century cottage is one of the rewards of an expedition to the furthest edge of Shropshire, beyond the Long Mynd. You have to read your map with great care to know if you are still in England or have ventured into Wales. The sturdy basket grate, with its cast-iron fireback, is of a type which owners of old buildings would do well to emulate. This was the first type of freestanding grate to be used when people ceased to burn logs on the hearthstone itself. Often the old fire-dogs would be retained and the grate perched on the horizontal billet bars, giving rise to the term 'dog grate'.

SHROPSHIRE

The often stated injunction that modern cottage dwellers should attempt to 'blend the old with the new' is exemplified by this daring 'kitchen unit', equally suited for bathroom use. The table and chair, with their ring-turned legs, look early Victorian. The closely spaced and generously thick ceiling joists appear to be original. Joists in 19th-century cottages tended to be of thinner and deeper section, and were generally placed wider apart.

HEREFORD AND WORCESTER

Not quite a cottage , more a late-18th-century farmhouse, but it was impossible to resist the messages from the past conveyed by that worn sandstone floor and the marvellous Victorian cast-iron range. To fit the range, the wide down-hearth has been bricked up on the left-hand side. The chimney crane is in its original position and from it hang an assortment of pothooks and a huge hot-water can with its own brass tap. This kitchen still is the place where family and farm hands eat their victuals. The apples on the table are 'Skulls', a local speciality.

HEREFORD AND WORCESTER

The farmhouse has a working kitchen today, while the original one is used for living and eating but not for cooking. In this picture, as if to order, the hens peck about the floor and jump on the table as they might have done in a cottage during the 18th century. The owners specialize in organic farming.

A 200-year-old painting on one of the plastered wall panels of a timber-framed Herefordshire cottage, near Leominster, has been confirmed by the Hereford Museum as genuine. The medium is egg tempora, and ground flower petals have been used as colour pigments. The scene is thought to be of Kew Gardens, which suggests that the lighthouse-like edifice in the background is Sir William Chambers's pagoda, although the resemblance is tenuous. In this cottage some of the wattle-and-daub infill has been left exposed, showing how split staves are sprung into the oak framing members and short lengths of wattle are woven across them. This provided the key for plaster made from earth and lime, reinforced with hair or chopped straw.

HEREFORD AND WORCESTER

Once the home of a smallholder with only a few acres of land, this mid-17th-century timber-framed building is now owned by an antique dealer. The chest of drawers, of roughly the same date as the house, is made from pine – an exceptionally early date for softwood to be used in cabinet-making. The big Staffordshire cow (*c.* 1830) says 'Milk Sold Here' on the base. It would have been used in a dairy window to advertise their wares. The view is from the hall to the parlour. Against the end wall is a little fall-front desk (*c.* 1740), also made of pine, with original wallpaper linings inside.

The parlour of the same cottage features a pretty Queen Anne oak lowboy with cabriole legs. On it is a pair of carved wooden boots, which were the work of a bootmaker's apprentice – an exercise designed to test his ability at making lasts. The spice cabinet of about 1680 has its original sludgy green paint and nailed butterfly hinges. The bizarre clock was made by a local sculptor from part of an old waggon. The face is of tin, bound in place with wire. It has a modern quartz movement and, by some strange alchemy, the pendulum has been made to move in unison with it. The Windsor chair is 18th century; the grain of its oak seat runs across the width.

GLOUCESTERSHIRE

The river valleys around Stroud in Gloucestershire are crammed with mills which serviced the wool trade upon which the area's prosperity was founded. A 17th-century miller's house like this one is of almost baronial substance, with its high ceiling, newel staircase and huge open hearth. The soft Cotswold limestone, while easy to work is also prone to wear, as the stair treads denote – each one is hollowed out in the exact position you automatically place a foot when going up or down. Originally the walls would have been plastered and the fireplace lintel, too, has been hacked to provide a key for plastering. Its great depth is required because of the inherent weakness of the stone. The plugged holes were probably for a mantel shelf and winding gear for spit-roasting.

GLOUCESTERSHIRE

Contemporary cottage owners can seldom afford to use the main areas of living space for kitchen purposes, as past generations would have done. Galley-like kitchens are therefore improvised in old sculleries, storerooms, lean-to dairies, outshuts and extensions. The former kitchen, with its big fireplace, often becomes the main living room and the parlour is usually added to it for good measure. This tiny kitchen of a Gloucestershire cottage can only be photographed by virtually sitting on the Aga cooker.

GLOUCESTERSHIRE

Gloucestershire buildings, however humble, can be far more sophisticated in detailing than their counterparts elsewhere. The easily worked limestone lends itself to embellishment. The porch of this small building, which is tucked into the side of a hill, is made of carefully dressed slabs no more than 6 inches thick, jointed with the accuracy of ashlar facing. The lintel has been cut to form an ogee profile – a medieval design which was re-adopted in the 17th century, and finally played its part in the various 18th- and 19th-century Gothic revivals.

The schoolmaster's house in a small Cotswold village is a curious blend of 17th-century vernacular building and medieval Gothic opulence. The lattice windows with their central mullions and cusped heads and the 'Early English' pointed arch of the porch are all, in fact, typical of mid-19th-century revival work in the manner of Pugin. The arched door on the right gives access to a passage which links the schoolrooms proper with the dwelling. Parish schools at the time were frequently laid out in this way and placed close to the church which founded them.

The present owners of the schoolmaster's cottage have harmonized their furnishing and decorations with the building but avoided being too zealously Gothic. The chairs echo the medieval pointed arches of the outside doors, and the '17th-century' elements are referred to in the bobbin turning of their uprights and rails. The fireplace with its distinctive corner blocks and roundels is of a type more usually encountered in early-19th-century houses. It has been painted with a stippled pattern to simulate marble.

Reflected in the gilt-framed mirror is what looks like an 18th-century fireplace with cornucopias on the frieze and a modern grate; but could the surround be late-Victorian painted cast-iron. The ebonized and gilded chairs are of Regency design, with backsplats formed from crossed spears. Such chairs were frequently made of beechwood. When the village schoolmaster lived here how much more dowdy might all this have been – ink-stained exercise books piled on horsehair sofas and chairs, and the inexorable odours of mutton and boiled cabbage.

GLOUCESTERSHIRE

Printed cotton curtains depicting pastoral scenes in the style of 18th-century *toile de Jouy* frame a pair of cusped windows. Through the leaded panes you can glimpse the rich farmland of rural Gloucestershire, which surrounds the schoolmaster's cottage. The transfer-printed jugs extol the virtues of diligent husbandry. The contents of the central one recalls the less worthy injunction: 'If you have a loaf of bread, sell half and buy lilies.'

GLOUCESTERSHIRE

This former inn, built in 1694, used to be a posting house at the western end of the Cotswolds. The picture is of the beer cellar, which forms a wing at the back of the inn. On the left, against the whitewashed wall, is a butler's tray with fold-up legs. The carpet is an Indian pattern made between the two World Wars. The portrait on the wall behind the chair is the owner's mother by the Edwardian painter Graham Glen, who also painted her father (an officer in the 20th Hussars).

Oxfordshire

The North Oxfordshire village of Bloxham is built of limestone containing the brown tinges of iron which give the masonry of the big open hearth in this early-17th-century workman's cottage its distinctive appearance. The chamfered spine beam and joists are original, and so is the wide oak-mullioned window, which would have once contained lead-glazed casements. The panelled shutters are 18th century and made of pine, while the back of the oak window seat is in elm. The oak wall shelves to the left of the window are late 17th century and described as a Delft rack – meant to house the tin-glazed earthenware which became so popular at that time. The village has its own carpet factory. The rug, which looks superficially like one of Persian medallion pattern, is an example of its work.

The kitchen of this cottage has been knocked through to make one room out of two. The ironstone pier supports the redistributed loads of beams and floor joists. The owners are keen winemakers and their vintages may be seen on the ledge and on the modern wax-polished tiled floor. Shelves made from English oak are filled with jars of spices, herbs and pulses. The English-oak dresser in the foreground was originally built *in situ* at a local manor house in the year 1680. The blue-and-white 19th-century plates on its shelves are transfer-printed with the immensely popular 'pheasant' design, which boasts a great deal more flowers than pheasants. The low, stool-like object is a gas-fired tailor's iron-heater containing its original irons, which slide out horizontally onto the ledge provided. The thumb latch screwed, not nailed, to the door (right) is a modern version of a very traditional type of fitting.

OXFORDSHIRE

A theatrical tableau
commands the stairhead in an
Oxfordshire cottage. The
owner worked as a designer
in television and the figures in
the washstand basin once
formed the background to the
titles of a programme. The
pictures, which are the work
of the owner, were exhibited
in a Chelsea theatrical
exhibition. The lampshade is
from the 1920s and was
bought in Amsterdam.

OXFORDSHIRE

This bedroom in the Oxfordshire cottage, not far from Chipping Norton, shows what can be done to maximize the use of roof space. The steeply sloping ceiling and old oak purlins lie beneath the thatch of an 18th-century building – part of a group, which includes at least one 17th-century dwelling. The sense of a canopy has been devised for the big brass bedstead – bought in a Glasgow market for £5. Striped cotton ticking has been swagged over a pole and trimmed with tassels, which echo the black lacquer mirror below.

BUCKINGHAMSHIRE

Records suggest that this extraordinary Buckinghamshire cottage existed in the 18th century, but how much older it could be is impossible to conjecture. It appears to be a tantalizing survivor from the days when poor farm workers were housed in tiny hovels, thrown up from whatever materials came to hand. The beams of entirely unconverted timber (possibly elm) seem to hold the crudely framed walls together. The billowing plaster ceiling is daubed onto a crazy mattress of twigs and branches which fills the roof space. The fireplace piers have been rebuilt with old bricks from the chimney. One inside the hearth is marked 'A.W. 1810'. The sitting room measures a minuscule 8 feet 3 inches by 12 feet and the 6-foot-tall owner can only stand upright in three places between the beams! The walls measure about 4 feet 3 inches to the wall plates. The left-hand wall has been rebuilt in clay lump and, unlike the framed one on the right, is leaning outwards.

Looking at the outside of this single-storey cottage, not far from Aylesbury, you would think it pretty but not remarkable. It has a combed wheat-reed roof and is obviously timber framed. The wing on the left is a modern addition, but the general impression, despite its newly built chimney, is that it might be dated around the early 19th century. The inside tells a far more intriguing story (see facing page and overleaf).

BUCKINGHAMSHIRE

The bedroom of the labourer's cottage near Aylesbury has the same original ceiling plaster, on a backing of twigs and branches, as the sitting room. The part from the beam to the window is about 4 feet 3 inches above the floor. An 18th-century addition has been made at the opposite end of the cottage, which now contains the kitchen. A modern extension under a thatched roof provides another bedroom and a bathroom. Some of the doors in the building are only 20 inches wide in places, causing frightful problems when moving furniture.

The hall of this ingenious cottage was added to the early nucleus by a local builder who specialized in the re-use of salvaged parts from other houses – many brought in from relatively far afield. This practice explains the somewhat surprising stained glass in the mullioned window above the serpentine-fronted chest of drawers. One diamond pane is etched with the three ostrich plumes of the Prince of Wales and his German motto 'Ich Dien', meaning 'I serve'. The other diamond has a fleur-de-lys. The glass is signed W. Doyle 1812.

BUCKINGHAMSHIRE

Only on very close inspection does this charming Buckinghamshire cottage reveal that it is not quite what it first appears. The leaded, mullioned windows, tumbled-brickwork panels, undulating tiled roof and jettied upper storey on the right, all imply a building of at least 17th-century vintage. The hip-roofed wing on the left, with windows tucked under the eaves, could even denote a medieval hall-house. However, much of the cottage, including the main entrance elevations, is apparently the adroit work of Thomas Quarterman, a specialist local builder who built a number of houses in this vein during the period between the wars. His forte was the re-use of materials from early buildings, which he dismantled and incorporated with cunningly contrived adaptations of his own devising. Evidence of such practices can be found, but are far from obvious.

At first sight this scene appears to represent a medieval hall with a central tie beam and a crown post rising from it, but in this diverting house nothing can be taken for granted. The high windows under the eaves are in the kind of position you might expect of an open hall, but the fireplace is not authentic and the timber studwork above it does not equate with the usual pattern of structural framing. Nonetheless, this is likely to be the original and early part of the building and the overall effect must be counted a success.

BUCKINGHAMSHIRE

Detectives of old buildings find one of the most revealing features of a cottage is the material from which the ground floors are constructed. The mellow and undulating polished tiles which provide welcome colour to the floor of this 16th-century dwelling are typical of Buckinghamshire. The longcase clock was made by W. Nicholas, Birmingham (1780–1825), and is of a type frequently seen in that period. The chair shows Chippendale influence, but the arms are of early-19th-century style.

The staircase of the cottage ascends in steep and narrow flights, the turns effected by the use of winders. Nothing else would produce that sweep of plaster overhead. With prehensile dexterity the practised inhabitants must swing from one iron handgrip to the next as they hurtle towards the ground floor.

HERTFORDSHIRE

HERTFORDSHIRE

The fireplace in this tiny timber-framed Hertfordshire cottage is a later addition, possibly constructed to accommodate the mid-19th-century kitchen range. The colour print over the fire is typical of the rather sentimental genre scenes of cottage life which often turn out to be painted by Francis Wheatley (1747–1801). This one depicts the bashful young suitor being inspected by the family of a demure but formidable damsel. Left of the fireplace is an early-19th-century Davenport desk.

Minute cottages as early as this one have nearly always been added to. The part to the left of the 19th-century chimney stack is the original late-16th-to-early-17th-century nucleus of the building . The stack was built to serve a fireplace in the parlour extension. The enormously tall chimney pot – all of 5 feet high – has been plonked on top to beat the downdraughts caused by the roof.

Photographer's Notes

As Hugh Lander was working his way round the English countryside in his van, comfortably equipped with armchair and potpourri, I and my assistant, Josh, were fitting out a large trailer with the vast assortment of equipment needed to photograph the darkest, tiniest and most inaccessible cottage interior.

Armed with sunlight and daylight lamps, flash equipment, a large assortment of cameras and lenses, black velvet, polystyrene reflector boards, stands, clamps and cases of film and polaroid materials, we set out on the first of a series of long journeys. With the aid of good maps and careful instructions we found our way to often remote places, along muddy cart tracks, through woods and over unmarked moorland to the many and varied cottages that are illustrated in this book. Many were extraordinary; their eccentricities occasionally mirrored by their occupants!

The cottage owners all showed us consideration and hospitality despite considerable inconvenience. Crammed into tiny corners of minuscule kitchens they would offer us advice, interest and mugs of coffee. As we moved furniture, pulled up carpets to expose ancient flagstones, bare earth or old floorboards, disconnected light fittings, hi-fis, fridges and storage heaters, still the coffee and conversation flowed with only the occasional anxious glance or question.

I have tried to make these pictures honest representations of the cottages visited, although at times a little trickery was employed. Evening sunlight can be seen streaming through a window that has no outlook and piles of books or cleverly positioned furniture obscure a radiator. The quirky combinations of old and new I have usually left untouched, so that an old stone sink sports a bright pair of Marigold gloves, garish plastic containers nestle amongst their earthenware counterparts and *The Sun* newspaper flourishes on an ancient kitchen table.

The exclusive use of natural light was not always possible. Fighting its way through tiny windows under low eaves and through dense foliage, it was no match for the dark walls, fireplaces and furniture. Boosting the existing daylight was achieved by positioning large polystyrene reflector boards outside doors and windows. These also helped to neutralize the colour casts created by green vegetation in the gardens. At times when light levels were too low for this technique, large soft-lights powered by electronic flash were used with the occasional addition of tungsten spot lamps to create a harder, sunnier effect. These lights were sometimes directed through suspended branches or 'gobos' to break up the hardness and create summery 'dapples'.

Internal lighting – in addition to the cosy glow of domestic lamps or candles – was difficult in such restricted areas but also proved essential in some circumstances. The warmth of firelight from hearths stacked high with dry kindling, sprinkled with barbeque lighting fluid, was enhanced with light bounced from hidden gold reflectors. Internal doors were left ajar so that lights positioned outside flooded in to illuminate the room.

PHOTOGRAPHER'S NOTES

When working in a small space filled with interesting clutter the initial temptation is to 'get it all in' by use of the wide-angle lens. This has several severe disadvantages as the exaggerated perspective makes foregrounds large and uninteresting whilst smaller details on a far wall recede into obscurity. An added problem is that a tiny cottage parlour begins to assume the proportions of a stately home. The only solution is to 'get back' with a longer lens. Photographing through open windows or doors was sometimes possible. Often I had to resort to Heath Robinson clamping devices in order to suspend cameras at the back of a cupboard, bookcase or stairwell. On occasions, when an awkward viewpoint was necessary and distortion was a problem, I would resort to a plate camera where the camera movements could be used to correct any visual imbalance.

Nothing, however, can correct the distortion created by the effects of time on old structures. As earth subsides and timbers shrink, doorways start to lean and floors slope. These are truly the properties of an old cottage and should not be blamed on the photographer's abilities!

Cameras used were Mamiya RB 6×7, lenses 50–250; Sinar P 5×4, lenses 65–480. Lighting: Broncolor 606 and 404 packs; Broncolor 'Quadroflex' diffusers; LTM 2kw spotlights; Ianiro 1kw spotlights. Film: Fujichrome 100 ASA (daylight), 64 ASA (tungsten); Ektachrome 64 ASA (daylight); Agfachrome 1000 ASA (daylight).

My thanks go to Sonya, my P.A., for her organizing skills, to Josh, my assistant, for being such good company throughout, and to all those cottagers who allowed me to capture the past. They have been patient and tolerant as well as delightful and informative.

GLOSSARY

ARCH-BRACE Curved timber which stiffens the junction between a principal rafter, its collar or tie beam and the main structural post upon which it rests. Often decorated with mouldings.

BAKING IRON A form of short-legged trivet, placed over the coals of the fire to support a girdle plate, upon which dough is baked.

BEAM A structural timber of substantial section mainly used to support floor joists or to tie the feet of two principal rafters together, thus forming a roof truss.

BOLECTION MOULDING Usually used around wall or door panels, but also fireplaces, this moulding stands proud of the framing members and is often shaped in a double curve or 'ogee'.

BOSS A carved or moulded ornamental block covering the intersection of beams or ceiling ribs.

BUTT PURLIN Purlins which are jointed into the sides of the principal rafters by means of mortices and tenons. Threaded purlins pass right through the rafters.

BOX FRAME Form of framed construction, consisting of sturdy posts and horizontal timbers, used for houses and cottages, especially in the 16th and 17th centuries. Roof trusses can be carried by both the vertical posts and the horizontal plates.

CASEMENT A window which is side-hung to open outwards in Britain, and inwards in European countries.

CAT-SLIDE ROOF The roof slope, usually at the back of a building, is continued downwards to cover a ground-floor extension or projection.

COLLAR Horizontal timber spiked or pegged to each pair of rafters to stop them pulling apart under load.

COMMON RAFTER A sloping roof timber which supports the roof covering of battens and tiles, slate or thatch. Rafters themselves rest upon purlins which bridge between main roof trusses.

CONTINUED CHIMNEYPIECE A large, classically inspired chimneypiece which extends right up the wall to form an architectural feature with bold cornice or pediment.

CORBEL A stone or timber support which projects from a wall to carry the load of a structural member such as a beam.

DOWN-HEARTH A fireplace in which the logs are burned on the hearthstone itself, without the use of a grate.

GABLE A triangular area of wall which fills or covers the space formed between the sloping roof timbers. Can also mean the entire gable end of a building.

GABLET Small triangle of wall at the peak of the roof with the tiles

of a hip slope running below it. Also an ornamental feature in other positions.

GIRDLE An iron plate upon which dough is placed over the fire when baking.

GRIP FLOOR Mixture of beaten lime and ash, normally used as a ground floor, but sometimes laid upstairs on laths supported by joists.

GUILLOCHE A decorative design of continuous interlacing circles.

HALL-HOUSE A building with a main ground-floor room, or hall, which rises the full height of the building to the roof space.

HIP ROOF One which has triangular roof slopes at each end, forming 'hips' where they join the main roof slopes.

H-L HINGE Typical 17th- and 18th-century hinge, consisting of two upright steel plates hinged together – one extended to form an L.

HOB GRATE Cast-iron coal-burning grate. Late 18th century onwards.

JETTIED A building is said to be jettied, when the timber framing of the upper storeys is made to jut out beyond the ground-floor walls.

LATTICE A lattice window is one which is glazed with diamond-shaped panes held by lead strips called 'cames', wooden or iron glazing bars. The term is derived from the use of diagonally set strips of timber used in unglazed windows – still occasionally seen in larders.

LEAD-GLAZING Window glass held in position by thin strips of lead called 'cames'. The panes are smaller than those used in windows with wooden glazing bars and are often diamond shaped.

MULLION Stone or timber upright, dividing window openings vertically into separate 'lights'.

MUNTIN The intermediate upright framing members in doors or panelling.

NEWEL A structural post in stone, metal or wood, supporting a balustrade at the top, bottom and changes of direction in a staircase.

OGEE MOULDING Moulding S-shaped in section – part convex, part concave.

OUTSHUT A relatively small extension projecting from a wall of a building, but normally covered by a continuation of the main roof slope. Usually formed to house staircases and small service rooms.

OVERMANTEL The upper part of a chimneypiece above the level of the mantel-shelf. Usually consists of a panel topped by a cornice or pediment, sometimes flanked by volutes or pilasters.

OVOLO Convex moulding, which in the case of a 'quadrant' describes a quarter circle.

PAMMENT Unglazed clay tiles, usually square, made in East Anglia for flooring.

PRINCIPAL RAFTER In a roof pairs of these form a series of 'trusses' carrying purlins, which in their turn, support the smaller common rafters. Often left exposed in attic rooms.

PURLIN Structural timber running lengthways along a roof, of roughly square section. Transfers load of common rafters to the roof trusses.

RAIL A horizontal framing member in door or panelling construction.

REGISTER GRATE A cast-iron or sheet metal plate fills the main fireplace opening. The plate itself has a diminished opening for a relatively small fitted grate. Normally second half of 19th century.

RIM LOCK Metal cased lock screwed or bolted to face of door.

RISER The vertical face of a step.

SCRATCH MOULDING Shallow decorative mouldings normally run on the framing members of oak furniture and panelling, but also used in other contexts. They are 'scratched' fairly close to the surface of the wood rather than cut deeply.

SOFFIT The underside of window openings, beams, etc.

STILE The outermost vertical framing members of a system of panelling, and in the same way, of a door.

STOPPED CHAMFER When the lower edge of a beam, for example, ceases to be chamfered off, it is said to be 'stopped'. For this purpose various decorative mouldings are used to effect the change from 'chamfer' to plain rectangular section.

STRETCHER Horizontally placed framing member used in furniture-making to stiffen and brace the legs.

STRING Thick wooden board placed in an upright position, into which the ends of the stair treads are housed. A closed string presents the sight of the string only, while a cut string allows you to see the outline of the steps.

STUD Vertical timber used to form the frame of a partition wall.

T-HINGE A relatively thin iron hinge consisting of an upright plate nailed to the door frame, while a long metal strap, running at right angles to it, is nailed to the door.

TIE Any structural timber which is used to hold other framing members together, rather than bracing them apart. Technically, it is in tension rather than in compression.

TRUSS Roof trusses consist of pairs of principal rafters, tied with a horizontal member to form a triangle.

FURTHER READING

Ayres, James *The Shell Book of the Home in Britain* (UK and USA Faber, 1981)

Batsford, Harry & Fry, Charles *The English Cottage* (UK Batsford, 1938, 3rd rev. edn. 1950; USA Scribner, 1939)

Brown, R.J. *The English Country Cottage* (UK Robert Hale, 1979; Hamlyn, 1984 pbk)

Brunskill, R.W. *Timber Building in Britain* (UK Gollancz, 1985)

Brunskill, R.W. *Illustrated Handbook of Vernacular Architecture* (UK Faber, 1970, 2nd rev. edn. 1978; USA Universe Books, 1970)

Burney, Fanny *Journals and Letters*, 12 vols (UK Clarendon Press, 1972)

Clifton-Taylor, Alec *The Pattern of English Building* (UK Faber, 1972)

Cobbett, William *Rural Rides* (UK Penguin, 1967)

Cunnington, Pamela *How Old is your House?* (UK Alphabooks, 1980)

Curl, James Stevens *English Architecture: An Illustrated Glossary* (UK David & Charles, 1977)

Delaney, Mary *Autobiography and Correspondence*, 3 vols (UK Richard Bentley, 1862; USA AMS Press Inc., reprint of 1862 edn.)

Dixon, Roger & Muthesius, Stefan *Victorian Architecture* (UK Thames & Hudson, 1978; USA Oxford University Press, 1978)

Fastnedge, Ralph *English Furniture Styles 1500–1830* (UK Penguin, 1955; USA Barnes, 1964)

Fiennes, Celia *The Journeys of Celia Fiennes* (UK Cresset Press, 1947; USA Chanticleer, 1949)

Fleming, John & Honour, Hugh *The Penguin Dictionary of Decorative Arts* (UK Penguin, 1977; USA Harper & Row, 1977)

Genders, Roy *The Cottage Garden and the Old Fashioned Flowers* (UK Pelham Books, 1969)

Hartley, Dorothy *Made in England* (UK Methuen, 1939; Century Pub., National Trust Classics, 1987; USA Saunders, 1939)

Holme, Charles (Ed.) *Old English Country Cottages* (UK Studio Office, 1906, special winter no. of the *Studio*)

Jervis, Simon *The Penguin Dictionary of Design and Designers* (UK Penguin, 1984)

Lander, Hugh *Do's and Don'ts, House & Cottage Interiors* (UK Acanthus Books, 1982)

Lander, Hugh *The House Restorer's Guide* (UK David & Charles, 1986)

Lindsay, John Seymour *An Anatomy of English Wrought Iron: 1000–1800* (UK Alec Tiranti, 1964; USA Taplinger, 1965)

Lindsay, John Seymour *Iron and Brass Implements of the English House* (UK Alec Tiranti, 1970; prev. edn. Medici, 1927; USA Clarke, 1964)

Lloyd, Nathanial *History of the English House* (UK Architectural Press, 1975; USA Antique Collectors Club, 1983)

Loudon, J.C. *Encyclopaedia of Cottage, Farm and Villa Architecture* (UK Longmans 1833; reissued S.R. Publishers, 1970)

Mercer, Eric *English Vernacular Houses* (UK HMSO, 1975)

Moritz, Carl Philipp *Journeys of a German in England in 1782* (UK Cape, 1965; USA Holt, 1965)

Mountfield, David *The Antique Collectors' Illustrated Dictionary* (UK Hamlyn, 1974)

Osborne, Harold (Ed.) *The Oxford Companion to Art* (UK Clarendon Press, 1970)

Owen, Michael *Antique Cast Iron* (UK Blandford, 1977)

Puckler-Muskau, Hermann *Puckler's Progress* (UK Collins, 1987)

Richardson, A.E. & Eberlein, H. Donaldson *The Smaller English House of the Later Renaissance 1660–1830* (UK Batsford, 1925; USA Helburn, 1925)

Rogers, John C. *English Furniture* (UK Spring Books, 1923; USA Scribner, 1923)

Scott, John S. *A Dictionary of Building* (UK Penguin, 1974)

Service, Alastair *Edwardian Architecture* (UK Thames & Hudson, 1977)

Teynac, F., Nolot, P. & Vivien, J.D. *Wallpaper: A History* (UK Thames & Hudson, 1883; USA Rizzoli, 1982)

Thompson, Flora *Larkrise to Candleford* (UK Penguin, Penguin Modern Classics, 1973)

Thornton, Peter *Authentic Decor: The Domestic Interior 1620–1920* (UK Weidenfeld & Nicolson, 1984; USA Viking Press, 1984)

West, Robert C. *Thatch* (UK David & Charles, 1987; USA Main Street, 1988)

Wood, Margaret *The English Mediaeval House* (UK Dent, 1965; USA Verry, 1965)

Woodforde, James *The Diary of a Country Parson, 1758–1802* (UK Oxford University Press, 1978)

Woodforde, John *The Truth about Cottages* (UK Routledge & Kegan Paul, 1969; USA Kelley, 1970)

Yarwood, Doreen *The British Kitchen* (UK Batsford, 1981)

Yarwood, Doreen *The English Home* (UK Batsford, 1956; USA Scribner, 1956)

INDEX

(*see also* Glossary, page 156)